4|30|00
$25.00
BuT
AS
4aa/

DATE DUE

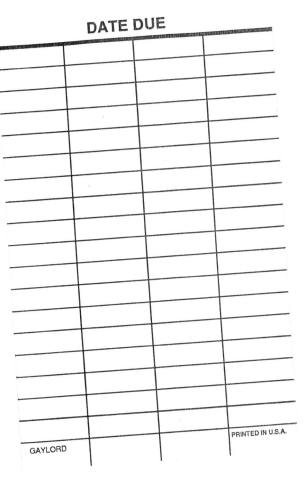

GAYLORD

PRINTED IN U.S.A.

Zydeco!

Photographs by Rick Olivier
Text by Ben Sandmel

University Press of Mississippi / Jackson

To the memory of

Clifton Chenier, who opened the door to his house
and the door to his world;
Samuel and Frances Sandmel and Jacob Marcus,
who would be so excited to see this; and
Irene Dugas Olivier, 1914-1998.

http://www.upress.state.ms.us

Photographs copyright © 1999 by Rick Olivier
Text copyright © 1999 by Ben Sandmel
All rights reserved
Manufactured in Canada

Designed by Todd Lape

02 01 00 99   4 3 2 1

The paper in this book meets the guidelines for permanence and durability
of the Committee on Production Guidelines for Book Longevity of the
Council on Library Resources.

Library of Congress Cataloging-in-Publication Data

Olivier, Rick.
    Zydeco! / photographs by Rick Olivier ; text by Ben Sandmel.
        p.   cm.
    Discography: p.
    Filmography and videography: p.
    Includes bibliographical references (p.   ) and index.
    ISBN 1-57806-115-6 (cloth : alk. paper). — ISBN 1-57806-116-4
(pbk. : alk. paper)
    1. Zydeco music—History and criticism. 2. Zydeco musicians—
Louisiana—Portraits.   I. Sandmel, Ben. II. Title.
ML3560.C2505   1999
781.62'410763—dc21   98-48793
                                                        CIP
                                                         MN

British Library Cataloging-in-Publication Data available

Right: Boozoo Chavis at Richard's Club, Lawtell, Louisiana
Frontispiece: p. 2, Mark Williams, fire frottoir
Overleaf: p. 6, Chris Ardoin at Spanish Lake near Prairieville, Louisiana;
pp. 8–9, Rockin' Dopsie and Dopsie, Jr. at the Maple Leaf Bar, New Orleans

Contents

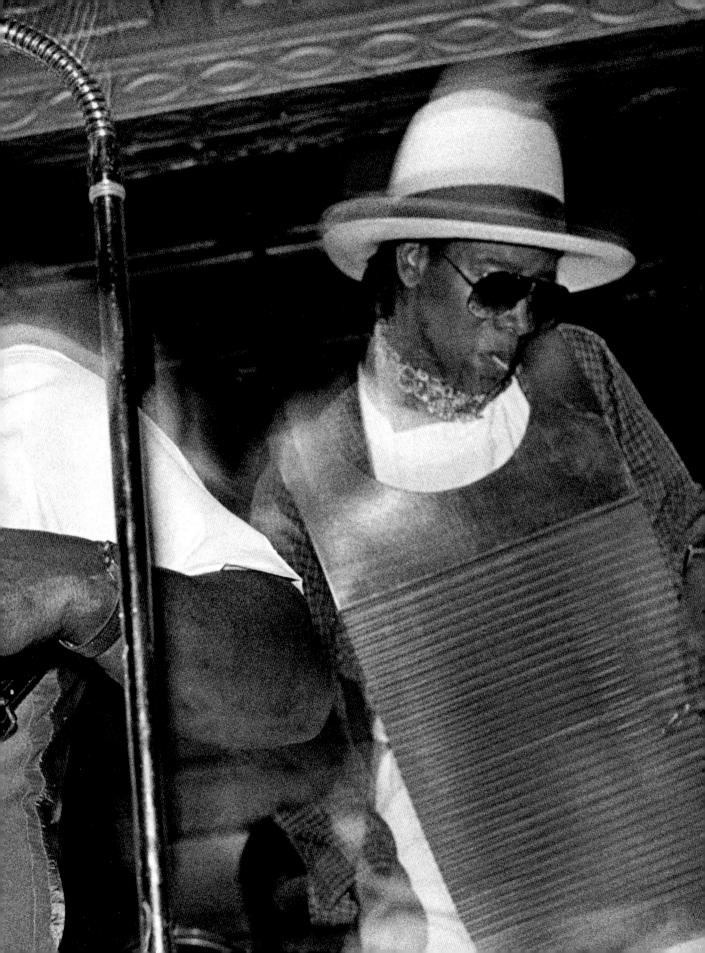

Zydeco!

Allons au Zydeco

The Place and the People

On Saturday nights in southwest Louisiana, a weekly ritual unfolds in the bars and clubs along the "crawfish circuit." Working men and women exchange their work clothes for plumed Stetsons and fancy dresses, and converge on rural roadhouses to dance to zydeco. Like the rough-and-tumble juke joints of the Mississippi Delta, few of these clubs maintain a slick appearance. Driving by in the daytime, one could easily assume that they closed down years ago and have languished in ramshackle neglect, their rutted and unpaved parking lots giving way to cane fields and pastures.

Come Saturday night those lots fill quickly, however, and many patrons must park a half-mile down the highway. It's well worth the walk for the rollicking scene that awaits inside. Against a backdrop of low ceilings, plain plank floors, and year-round Christmas lights, the mood rises to fever pitch as zydeco bands play marathon four-hour sets. These groups are led by an accordionist, who is apt to incite the crowd by playing on his knees, behind his back, or even on the floor, limbo-style—a move which inspires shouts of *"fais 'tention!"* ("watch out, now!") and "go ahead on!" Then the accordionist "breaks it down," playing a frenzied double-time solo accompanied only by the drums and a "rubboard." Tireless couples dance on to sweaty euphoria, because zydeco rivals oil as Louisiana's most potent source of energy.

Through most of the twentieth century such fervor unfolded as part of a self-contained community tradition—first at private "house parties" and then at local dance halls during the decades that followed World War II. By the early 1960s, zydeco's popularity had plummeted. Dismissed as "old folks' music," it was scorned as hopelessly passé and embarrassingly ethnic in an era of rigid conformity. Zealots such as the late Clifton Chenier, zydeco's single most important artist, kept the music alive during this lean period. Chenier was supported by a core of loyal followers at home and by enclaves of expatriate Louisianans in Texas and California. Even so, these were tough times for musicians who played the accordion and sang in French.

Some twenty years later, Louisiana's cultural climate had changed completely. Diversity had become acceptable, if not downright chic, as had personal ex-

Preceding page: Jimmy Serile, frottoir on the floor at Slim's Y-Ki-Ki, Opelousas, Louisiana

ploration of ethnic roots and heritage. This boded well for traditional music, and three zydeco artists won Grammy awards in quick succession—California's Queen Ida in 1982, Clifton Chenier in 1984, and Rockin' Sidney in 1986. Spurred by these and other mainstream affirmations, zydeco's exciting sound leapt into public consciousness. Today, on the brink of the millennium, zydeco is routinely featured in national television commercials, on motion picture sound tracks, and at live performances around the world. The Internet hosts numerous zydeco Web sites where nuggets of information about musicians, performances, dance steps, and new albums are instantly and avidly disseminated.

Homegrown zydeco events that once drew only local crowds now bring in throngs of tourists, while a network of clubs and festivals offers steady employment for zydeco bands on tour.

The word "zydeco" has also taken on expanded associations. Now considered a symbol of dynamism, the term appears on restaurant menus, as the name of an oil-and-gas exploration company, and on products as diverse as computer software and tandem bicycles. Most significantly, zydeco — which came perilously close to extinction — has reemerged as the music of choice for young people within its community of origin. At zydeco shrines such as Slim's Y-Ki-Ki in Opelousas, the Dauphine Club in Parks, and Richard's (pronounced REE-shard's) in Lawtell, the dance floor is packed with couples of all ages, leaving no room for thoughts of a generation gap. Once taken for granted or shunned, southwest Louisiana's unique ethnicity now inspires pride, celebration, and unity.

The photographs, commentary, and oral history that appear in *Zydeco!* were gathered during this heady time of transformation. Before then, this work might never have been commissioned. But despite the far-flung reaches of zydeco's ever-expanding domain, southwest Louisiana is still the wellspring for such vital music. In this book, Rick Olivier and I focus on the home front — the complex regional culture that forged zydeco — and look at the changes that continue to influence the music's evolution. Since oral tradition has always fueled zydeco's development, its practitioners and participants speak at length here in their own words.

Zydeco (pronounced ZY-duh-coe) is the exuberant dance music of southwest Louisiana's black Creoles. Stylistically, it is a rich hybrid, with a core of Afro-Caribbean rhythms, blues, and Cajun music (zydeco's white counterpart), and a wealth of other elements that may vary widely from band to band. Traditionally, zydeco is sung in French, and its lyrics are often improvised. It is absolutely not intended for passive listening. As Clifton Chenier stated, "If you know how to dance, then you can dance behind someone beating on an old gallon bucket. But if you can't dance to zydeco, you can't dance, period."

The word "zydeco" is often explained as an elision of the French phrase *"les haricots"* (pronounced lay-ZAH-ree-coe). The phrase *"les haricots sont pas salés"* appears frequently in black Creole folk music. Literally translated "the snapbeans are not salty," it is also a metaphor for times so hard that people cannot afford salt pork to season their food. Heard in many traditional songs, this phrase gradually generated several separate yet related meanings: the title of a song, "Zydeco sont pas salés"; the name of the musical genre represented by that song; the social gatherings where such music was played; and the dance steps and the act of dancing that the music inspired. These overlapping definitions can be perplexing, and journalist Susan Orlean astutely pointed out that "[i]n theory, this meant you could zydeco to zydeco at the zydeco." In this book, however, "zydeco" refers specifically to music.

The terms "Creole" and "Cajun" appear here often. "Creole" is a highly controversial word in south Louisiana, involving a complex, biased web of racial and socioeconomic identities. In a dispassionate, academic sense, "Creole" refers to people of old-world ancestry who were born in the new world. This broad definition was also used in the Caribbean, offering one example of south Louisiana's status as the northern frontier of Caribbean culture. Such connections are also reflected in the state's culinary, architectural, linguistic, and musical traditions.

In this book, "Creole" refers to the members of southwestern Louisiana's black community who speak French or have ancestors who did. These are the people who created zydeco. "Cajun" refers to their white, French-speaking neighbors. This definition of "Creole" is a subjective usage that neither endorses nor dismisses other interpretations. The "Creole" debate is likely to rage on, unresolved, throughout south Louisiana. Many people who call themselves "Creole," by whatever definition, become livid when the name is used by others whom they consider inferior, unworthy usurpers. A brief look at some of the other meanings shows why the term is so volatile.

In Louisiana, "Creole" was first used in the eighteenth century to describe the descendants of European colonists. Specifically, it often designated old-line white families of French and Spanish ancestry, many of whom were en-

Above: Rice field with crawfish traps near Church Point, Louisiana
Right: Prairie sunset near Opelousas, Louisiana

sconced in plantation society. These "Creoles" considered themselves quite distinct from *les américains*—a disdainful term for the English-speaking whites who arrived from points north via the Mississippi River and the Natchez Trace. Contradiction and controversy attended even this early definition, however, since "Creole" slave owners sometimes applied the term to slaves of African descent who were born in Louisiana.

During the eighteenth century many wealthy white "Creoles" were dismayed to see "Creole" emerge as a term for light-skinned black people, many of whom also spoke French, and who traced their ancestry to the Caribbean. Some of these "Creoles" had been brought to Louisiana as slaves, while others emigrated as "free people of color" following the Haitian revolution of 1791, when Haiti became the new name for the former French colony of Saint-Domingue. Among these latter emigrants was a significant number of educated professionals. Their presence was especially threatening to those whites who lived in fear of a slave rebellion.

There was also considerable friction between the light-skinned black "Creole" community and darker African Americans who spoke English and bore Anglo surnames. Such hostility lingers today, and may flare up during political campaigns when dark-skinned black candidates accuse "Creole" competitors of actually being white. Finally, the word may be applied in a completely different, noncontroversial way to native or homegrown items, such as "Creole" tomatoes. This kind of usage, as prevalent as it is seemingly frivolous, significantly compounds the confusion.

The late New Orleans blues guitarist Boogie Bill Webb once offered his explanation of "Creole" to folklorist Nick Spitzer: "[T]hey call it Creole to keep the black boy from being a white boy . . . Ain't no damn such thing as no Creole." The touchy ambiguity of Webb's personal definition underscores the point that "Creole" has become an indefinable buzzword. Almost everyone has an opinion, but there is little consensus.

The term "Cajun" has fewer racial ambiguities. Referring to white people, it is a shortened form of "Acadian." The Acadians were residents of Acadie, a prosperous French colony in what is now Nova Scotia. Britain took control of

Acadie in 1713, as the initial phase of its ultimate colonization of Canada. The British were then faced with the question of what to do with the Acadians, who were successfully farming the region's best land. This left newly arriving British settlers with the daunting task of carving out homesteads from the wilderness. There were also concerns that Acadians might help France in the ongoing struggle for Canadian dominance. In 1755 Britain finally solved its problems by deporting the Acadians, who embarked on a long and torturous search for a new homeland. It was a deeply traumatic experience that has left a cultural legacy of clannish self-protection. After a series of chilly receptions along the eastern seaboard, many of the exiles eventually established a series of remote settlements that began some one hundred miles west of New Orleans and extended on toward Texas.

This part of Louisiana remained isolated and self-contained until the end of the nineteenth century, allowing the Cajuns and Creoles to develop close-knit ethnic communities. Although markedly similar in many respects, the two groups were still distinguished by their disparate ancestry. Both cultures, in turn, were quite separate from the urbane French society of New Orleans. The Cajuns were not wealthy, as a rule, and did not maintain vast plantations; those who could afford slaves typically did not own very many, and usually toiled in the fields alongside them. Beyond the cruel and crucial difference of enslavement, blacks and whites in the region generally shared a hardscrabble rural existence that enhanced the development of dual traditions, including music. The similarity of their circumcumstances intensified with emancipation and the economic chaos of Reconstruction. Few Cajuns enjoyed a lifestyle of white linen suits and mint juleps on the veranda. In fact, the Cajuns were often scorned as "white trash" and endured considerable prejudice, which lingers today in the term "coon ass." Some Cajuns use this word amongst and in reference to themselves, but may bristle if it is uttered by others, much like the status of "nigger" for many African Americans.

At the turn of the twentieth century, Creole and Cajun country experienced a dramatic increase in contact with the outside world. Exploration for oil reserves began around 1900, followed by the ambitious system of new roads and

Roy Carrier's "Jr. Love" accordion

bridges that was built during the thirties by Governor Huey P. Long. Both were accompanied by an influx of workers from other areas, although locals were also employed. Sweeping social change accompanied such accelerated access, which was further spurred by the advent of radio and the record industry. In terms of musical development this gave Creoles and Cajuns increased exposure to nationally popular styles and commercial trends.

In the mass media, New Orleans and Creole/Cajun country are often depicted as one contiguous region, despite cultural contrasts and geographic separation. Culinary traditions in the two areas are markedly different, for instance; a New Orleans gumbo can be quite bland when compared to its fierce country cousin from Lafayette or Opelousas. And some five hundred thousand people in southwest Louisiana still speak and sing in Creole or Cajun French — although most are equally fluent in English — while French has vanished from the streets of New Orleans, except for a few isolated words and phrases.

Another popular misconception depicts Cajun/Creole country as one vast and exotic bayou, teeming with alligators and accessible only by boat or *pirogue*. In reality there are few people out in the swamps, and little musical activity. Most of the region is a vast expanse of flat farmland known as the prairies, and this includes the heart of the zydeco circuit. Rice, soybeans, and sugarcane are the principal crops. The subtle beauty of this countryside has inspired many contemporary artists, such as the noted landscape painter Elemore Morgan, Jr., and Francis X. Pavy, whose canvasses encompass both the physical terrain and the cultural realm, including music. Noted writers of fiction who have set their work in these surroundings include Ernest Gaines, E. Annie Proulx, and Tim Gautreaux.

Cajun and Creole country's principal city is Lafayette. A hundred and thirty miles west of New Orleans, it is a cosmopolitan town of some one hundred thousand people, with a vibrant arts community and the intellectual resources of the University of Southwestern Louisiana. Lafayette and the surrounding countryside have embraced every aspect of modern communication and con-

sumerism, including the Internet, cable TV, vast shopping malls, and fast food franchises. This homogeneity makes it all the more remarkable that such an individualistic regional culture has survived and blossomed. Preservation is easy enough in the absence of options, but not when bland assimilation is just a Wal-Mart away.

Like Creole and Cajun culture, zydeco and Cajun music have much in common, but they are hardly identical. Folklorist Barry Ancelet succinctly described their interaction: "Cajuns learned style from black Creoles, and black Creoles learned repertoire from Cajuns." Both genres feature the accordion as the dominant instrument, with accompaniment by guitar, bass, and drums. (A few Cajun accordionists, such as Eddie LeJeune, are backed only by acoustic guitar and fiddle.) Zydeco often features the saxophone as a solo vehicle, and may also include full horn sections, although brass instruments are rare in Cajun music. Zydeco's notable sax soloists include John Hart, Allen "Cat Roy" Broussard, and the late Lionel Prevost. The fiddle, once prominent in zy-

Cleveland Chenier plays his frottoir with bottle openers

deco, has largely disappeared. It is still a key component in Cajun music, as is the pedal steel guitar, which would adapt well to zydeco, yet curiously did not cross over. But the electric guitar is a vital force in zydeco—more so than in Cajun music—as evidenced by such accomplished soloists as Paul "Little Buck" Senegal, Harry Hypolite, and Chester Chevalier. Zydeco and Cajun bands favor many of the same songs, such as "Jolie Blonde" ("Pretty Blonde") and "Allons à Lafayette" ("Let's Go to Lafayette"), which are primarily sung in French. Other numbers are essentially exclusive to one tradition or the other, and both genres have a long list of familiar favorites that bands are expected to play on request.

The two styles have also contributed to a south Louisiana genre known as "swamp pop"—a hybrid of pop, rock, and rhythm and blues performed by Cajun and Creole artists and recorded primarily during the 1950s and 1960s. In terms of structure and instrumentation, swamp pop is virtually identical to the era's pop, rock, and rhythm and blues (also known as R&B) found in other parts of the country. Accordions were rarely heard, for instance, and the use of French was similarly limited. Swamp pop's regional identity came instead from its soulful, emotional vocal style, which has clear antecedents in zydeco and Cajun music. Swamp pop yielded several national hits; "Sea of Love," a 1959 recording by Phil Phillips, is the best known and most frequently "covered" (recorded again by other artists). Creole and Cajun musicians often worked together on swamp pop records, where stylistic divisions between zydeco and Cajun music, such as the presence of horn sections, did not exist. Many zydeco and Cajun artists have also pursued careers in swamp pop, and still retain it in their repertoires. There is also a dedicated core of Creole and Cajun musicians who focus on swamp pop exclusively.

Zydeco stands apart from Cajun music and swamp pop in its Afro-Caribbean

T. Black with his piano accordion at Richard's Club

folk roots and rhythms. It also draws heavily on such mainstream African-American styles as blues, soul, rhythm and blues, and, lately, rap music. Elements of rock, country, and reggae may also appear. Zydeco tempos tend to be more assertive and syncopated than those heard in Cajun music, and zydeco drummers have far more leeway to let loose. This propulsive style, reminiscent of such contemporary Afro-Caribbean genres as zouk or soca, is highlighted by the startling use of dynamic flourishes that may explode without warning in the middle of a vocal passage or an instrumental solo. Oblivious to prevailing standards of song structure and percussive punctuation, this aggressive approach dramatically intensifies the music's energy level. It has even inspired the name of a zydeco band—Fernest and the Thunders, led by accordionist Fernest Arceneaux.

Zydeco's rhythmic textures are further enhanced by the *frottoir*, or rubboard—a corrugated metal vest that hangs from the shoulders and is scraped against the chest with spoons or bottle openers. This rasping sound is thought to reflect the influence of both African and Native American percussion instruments on Creole music. The *frottoir* can also be traced directly to a common household item, the washboard, which provided the rhythm for such African-American folk genres as jug band music. A washboard must be played by someone who is sitting down, however, which detracts from a band's stage presence. The Chenier brothers, Clifton and Cleveland, solved this problem by inventing the *frottoir* in the 1950s and having the first one made to order at a sheet-metal shop in Lafayette. Cajun music's main percussion instrument has traditionally been the far less dynamic *'tit fer* (little iron), or triangle, although its prominence has faded outside of traditional acoustic-music circles.

Although Cajun music has experienced considerable interaction with Anglo-American country music, it is much more than

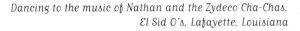

Dancing to the music of Nathan and the Zydeco Cha-Chas,
El Sid O's, Lafayette, Louisiana

Zydeco dancers at Hamilton's Club, Lafayette, Louisiana
Dancing couple at Slim's Y–Ki–Ki

country sung in French. Quite apart from Anglo tradition and Grand Ole Opry chauvinism, Cajun music also includes a wealth of Acadian and French folk material, some of which has medieval roots. These songs have significantly influenced zydeco, but zydeco has also incorporated such conventional, commercial country hits as "Last Date" and "Release Me."

Two distinct types of accordion are used in zydeco: diatonic models, which only play the full-step intervals found in major scales, and chromatic "piano" accordions, which encompass half-step intervals including "blue notes"—the flatted third and fifth of any given key. Diatonic accordions may be built to encompass one, two, or three keys—for progressively sophisticated players—and are classified accordingly as single-row, double-row, or triple-row models. Many Cajun accordionists incorporate half-steps and blue notes by playing in a different key from the tonic chord of their instrument, and more rows give them more options to do so. By custom, however, the chromatic piano accordion is rarely played in Cajun bands, except by modern groups such as Steve Riley and the Mamou Playboys, which use it only for the zydeco segments of their performances.

These distinctions between zydeco and Cajun music (and swamp pop) are guidelines rather than hard-and-fast rules. Cajun musicians have always been influenced by African-American blues, for instance, both through direct contact with black people and through the blues-influenced country hits of Jimmie Rodgers, Bob Wills, and Hank Williams. In a similar spirit of interchange, the repertoires of many rural zydeco artists such as Willis Prudhomme are steeped in Cajun waltzes, while zydeco's Delafose dynasty has a penchant for performing country songs. In recent years the lines have blurred even more dramatically. Cajun modernist Wayne Toups calls both his music and his band ZydeCajun, and incorporates many of zydeco's supercharged rhythms, as well as showing the influence of such southern-rock greats as the Allman Brothers. Today it's not unusual to see a *frottoir* player in a Cajun band or even in a video by rock star John Cougar Mellencamp.

These exceptions underscore the broader point that terminology has innate limitations in the world of traditional music. While useful as a point of reference, terminology is usually superimposed upon music long after its emergence. As such it is often imprecise, arbitrary, and overlapping, with nomenclature that changes continually over time. Also, the assigning of such categories is often irrelevant—if not annoying—to working musicians who actually play for a living. So are the related issues of purism and authenticity that spark heated debate on the sidelines. These questions are particularly murky in the case of zydeco, which has always been a hybrid.

There are two nearly absolute terms in south Louisiana, however. "Cajun music" is played by white bands, while "zydeco" refers to the sounds created by their Creole counterparts. But even this distinction is blurred by the fact that many Cajun and zydeco bands alike refer to their sound as "French music," while some zydeco musicians describe themselves as "black Cajuns." This is a politically incorrect oxymoron by contemporary standards, but it persists nonetheless. "Black Cajun" still appears in the press—most often, ironically, in southwest Louisiana—and the term can even be heard on an album by zydeco's definitive artist, Clifton Chenier.

The Emergence of Zydeco

Clifton Chenier:
"They Call Me the King"

A dozen years after his death, Clifton Chenier is still regarded as zy-deco's best-known and most influential musician. Such stature is unlikely to change. An agile, inventive accordionist and a passionate singer, Chenier pioneered contemporary zydeco, opened the door to global recognition for his protégés, and left a legacy of recordings that have set the standard for all who follow. He is reverently referred to as "the king" by his colleagues and disciples.

Clifton Chenier's most immediately noticeable trait was keen intelligence. He emanated a shrewd and vehement vigilance reminiscent of the renowned defense attorney F. Lee Bailey. Vivid though this first impression was, it took a good while to gather, because setting up a meeting with Clifton Chenier was no simple matter. In March of 1983 the magazine *Louisiana Life* sent me to Lafayette to interview Chenier and research a feature article about him. It would be my first interview with a zydeco musician and my first writing assignment from a local publication after arriving in New Orleans from Chicago several months before.

Despite his renown, Clifton Chenier did not have an office, a secretary, or an answering service. He handled all of his own business, in classic old-school fashion, and he was very difficult to reach by phone. For a month or so I tried to catch him every couple of days, always unsuccessfully, and Chenier's wife kept suggesting, "Why you don't call back." This south Louisiana syntax was jarring to a recent emigré, and I wondered whether she was actually asking me a question.

I finally talked to Chenier in person in New Orleans, and we agreed that I would come see him in Lafayette on the following Monday. At the appointed hour I went to his house on Magnolia Street, only to have his wife crack open the door and say, "Cliff ain't here"—even though he was standing right behind her. Repeat performances of these machinations were followed by a formal postponement so that Chenier could get his hair done for the photos that would accompany the article. It was Friday afternoon before we finally sat down to talk in his living room.

Then came the question of money. Chenier wanted five hundred dollars to do the interview—a reasonable request, really, since the chances were slim that yet another magazine article would bring him any indirect income or enable him to raise his fees. I told him that I simply didn't have it, and that *Louisiana Life* would not reimburse me. Chenier asked if I was getting paid to write the story, and I said yes. He paused, sizing me up, and then said, "Okay, go ahead. I just don't like bullshit. People come here from all over the world, and they try to tell me they ain't making no money." "The king" proceeded to give me an articulate, expansive interview . His life story illuminated zydeco's roots and its bright future. But when the cassette reached the end of side one, he wouldn't let me flip it. *"C'est tout,"* he said. "That's all. You got what you came for."

"I'm born and raised in Opelousas in 1925," Chenier began. "Outside of Opelousas. I come from out a hole, man, I mean out the *mud,* they had to dig me out the mud to bring me into town. You know, a lot of people don't like to say where they come from. But it ain't where you come from, man, it's what you *is.* The average fella now that's big stars, that's where they come from, out in the country."

Chenier never claimed zydeco as a personal invention, but he was well aware of his vital contributions. "The old generation had it," he explained, "but it died out. I brought zydeco back." What "the old generation had" was a blend of blues, French and Acadian material, and traces of Native American music, galvanized by Afro-Caribbean rhythms. This combination was expressed most dramatically in a tradition known as *juré* singing. *Juré* comes from the French *jurer*—to testify or swear—and is closely related to such archaic folk traditions as the African-American ring-shout and the Acadian *danse-ronde.* As with these styles, there was no instrumental accompaniment in *juré.* Hands and feet pounded out an urgent, primal beat—not unlike a fast rhumba or mambo, with added polyrhythms—while vocalists sang both secular and sacred lyrics.

There is no documentation as to just when *juré* emerged. But it has strong similarities to the antebellum music that was played at slave gatherings at Congo Square in New Orleans and described in detail by nineteenth-century journalists. It's quite possible that the two traditions are contemporaneous. Some stunning *jurés* were recorded by folklorist Alan Lomax for the Library of Con-

gress in 1934; besides containing riveting performances, these recordings mark the first documentation of the exclamation *"les haricots sont pas salés."*

Lomax called *juré* "the most African sound I found in America," and many first-time listeners are surprised to learn that these exotic recordings were really made on this continent. At the same time, some *juré* songs had distinct Acadian roots, and used melodies from popular Cajun songs that in turn drew on Anglo-American country music. One example is "Je fait tout le tour du pays" ("I Went All 'Round the Land,") the most striking *juré* in Lomax's collection. The title and theme come from an Acadian folk song, while parts of the melody resemble the Cajun favorite "J'étais au bal hier soir" ("I Went to the Dance Last

Alphonse "Bois-sec" Ardoin at home near Mamou, Louisiana

Night"). "J'étais au bal . . ." is based on the country song "Get Along, Cindy," and some bands play the two together as a French-English medley. Today, *juré* has all but vanished from oral tradition within the Creole community, but it is occasionally performed by musicians who have usually absorbed it from the Lomax recordings. A case in point is the Cajun band BeauSoleil, while a notable exception is accordionist Lynn August, a zydeco modernist who learned *juré* from his grandparents.

The Creole countryside where Clifton Chenier was raised was also permeated by European traditions. "We used to have two-steps, one-steps, waltzes, jigs, *contredanses*," Alphonse "Bois-sec" Ardoin told fellow accordionist Marc Savoy, in an interview conducted in French. Ardoin, one of Creole music's most important cultural ambassadors, was born in 1914, and raised in the far-flung region between Eunice and Basile. ("Bois-sec" is a nickname that literally means "dry wood.") This environment was very similar to the rural neighborhood on the fringes of Opelousas that Chenier had described as "out the *mud*." "The violin played all that," Ardoin continued. "That's what the people wanted. It's all forgotten now." These forms all contributed to the styles that would eventually come to be known as zydeco and Cajun music.

A crucial factor in their emergence was the accordion, which was brought to America from Germany and Austria. Peddlers sold the instrument in south Louisiana after the Civil War, and it caught on quickly. As Barry Ancelet observed, the accordion arrived "without instructions," giving the Creoles and Cajuns free reign to develop their own musical ideas. The accordion was durable, could be heard over noisy crowds, and worked well with a wide variety of styles. Continuing west, itinerant vendors also introduced the accordion into Texas, where it was welcomed in German and Czech communities and then adapted by Mexican-Americans to create the sound now known as *norteno* or *conjunto.*

One of south Louisiana's first great accordionists and recording artists was a black Creole named Amédé Ardoin. Ardoin made a series of seminal commercial recordings in the 1920s and 1930s, and there is strong debate today over whether they are appropriately classified as Cajun music or zydeco. Since both terms were coined later, the argument is academic. It is clear that Ardoin's inspired musicianship—expressed in a seamless, soulful blend of two-steps, blues, and waltzes—played a crucial role in forging both nascent schools. Ardoin's legacy still resonates today, in terms of style and repertoire, and also through the fourth-generation activity of his descendants. These include his nephew, Bois-sec, his sons Lawrence and Morris, and Bois-sec's grandson, Chris Ardoin, who leads a popular zydeco band called Double Clutchin'. Chris Ardoin's full, electrified band bursts with youthful enthusiasm but does not surpass the power of Amédé Ardoin's recordings, which jump across the decades with their passion and urgency.

Amédé Ardoin's records influenced young Clifton Chenier, as did the hit 78s of such acoustic blues artists as pianist and guitarist William Bunch, who recorded under the macho moniker "Peetie Wheatstraw, the Devil's Son-in-Law." Chenier was equally inspired by live performances. His father, Joseph, occasionally played a single-row accordion at house parties—until Clifton's mother slashed its bellows with a razor, disabling the instrument and presumably achieving the goal of ending her husband's career. Another family musician was Clifton's uncle, Morris Chenier, who played fiddle and guitar, and would later appear on some of his nephew's early records. But Clifton's best opportunities to learn came by watching and listening to such friends of the family as accordionists Claude Faulk, Jesse and ZoZo Reynolds, and Sidney Babineaux.

"I listened to Claude and the Reynolds a lot," Chenier told guitarist and researcher Ann Allen Savoy. "They had an old Model A Ford with a rumble seat in the back. So when they'd pass by my daddy's house to go play a dance I'd jump in that back seat, that little rumble seat. And when they'd get where they'd gone to play I'd get out the car. They couldn't do nothing, it was too far for me to walk back. I'd stay with 'em and listen to 'em. I was about eight or nine."

The young stowaway listened to music that was known in the 1930s by such names as "la-la," "pic-nic," and "bazar." "Zydeco" was still just a phrase heard in various songs, and not yet applied to the entire genre. Like zydeco in years to come, la-la incorporated elements of Afro-Caribbean *juré*, blues, Cajun mu-

Canray Fontenot in his backyard, Welsh, Louisiana

sic, and the European forms described by Bois-sec Ardoin. It was played for private gatherings more than at public dances. Creoles and Cajuns alike had a tradition of "house parties," where several extended families would take turns gathering at someone's home. Furniture would be moved aside to create a dance floor, and a weekend of fun would begin. La-la did not entail the full bands that perform zydeco today; it might be played by a lone accordion, an accordion and a washboard (the *frottoir* as such had yet to emerge), and perhaps a fiddle or a harmonica.

Sadly there are few recordings, either commercial or folkloric, that can document the contemporaneous development of la-la, although Cajun music has been recorded prolifically since the late 1920s. Those tracks that do exist can be heard on *Early Zydeco,* on Arhoolie Records, a Bay Area label with an extensive catalogue of south Louisiana music. But there are some great sessions from the 1960s and 1970s, by Bois-sec Ardoin and fiddler Canray Fontenot, which harken back to this era. They appear on Arhoolie and on two anthologies of field recordings produced by Nick Spitzer for the Rounder and Maison de Soul labels. Spitzer's recordings also feature additional members of the Ardoin family, the old-time fiddlers BéBé and Eraste Carrière, and Delton Broussard, the patriarch of another important musical family.

The limits of musical terminology are evident again in the insistence of both Fontenot and Ardoin that their rural style should be called *"la musique créole."* They refused to identify with the term "zydeco," and had doubts that anyone else should, either. As Fontenot told radio producer Jerry Embree:

They never had no such thing as zydeco music. No such thing as zydeco music. That's bullcorn. If you was black, you played Creole, if you was white, you played Cajun. They had a thing they called *juré.* The old people would sing for the young people, and clap their hands and make up a song. And they had a song about *"zaricots,"* *"zydeco,"* that's snap beans. Singin' about *"zaricots est pas salés,"* that's "snap beans with no salt in it." But I never saw one of them *juré* things.

I met Clifton Chenier once and he asked me, "Canray, you ever went to one of them *juré?"* and I said, "No, did you?" He said, "No, I never went to one, but my daddy used to

go. My daddy played the *'zaricots est pas salés'* on his accordion, but he didn't play it the right speed, he played it like a *juré.* I thought it should go faster."

Clifton told me, "I think I'm gonna make that *'zaricots est pas salés'* on a record, but I'm going to put some speed to it." He went and made that record, and after people found out that our type of music was moving, everyone wanted to have an accordion, and everyone wanted to play Clifton's stuff. But they don't know what they talkin' about when they talkin' about zydeco music, 'cause there's no such thing as that.

Having made this pronouncement, Fontenot then modified it slightly with a broader interpretation.

Willie Davis and van showing alternate spelling of zydeco

Zydeco mean another thing, too. If we had a dance in our neighborhood, maybe we couldn't invite some people from the other neighborhoods, 'cause then there'd be too many people to fit in the house. So we couldn't let everybody know. But they had to have some girls there, or then maybe nobody wouldn't come at all. So what they would do when they were going to have a dance, first thing, two guys would go out on horseback and start inviting people where they had some girls, to make sure some girls would come. But they would invite them to a "zydeco" so the other people from the neighborhood wouldn't know what they was talkin' about. It was like a secret word, 'cause they didn't want all them people showing up.

But they never had no such thing as zydeco *music*. Not as far as I know. If you was black, you played Creole.

In 1947 Clifton Chenier's music was still known as la-la. He moved from Opelousas to Lake Charles, Louisiana, a bustling petrochemical town just thirty miles east of the Texas border, and took a day job at the Gulf Oil refinery. Chenier's passion for music led to impromptu performances during his lunch break; at closing time he played for tips by the front gate, while his coworkers left for the day. Young, ambitious, and attracted to new ideas, Chenier began performing in public. He expanded the parameters of la-la by adding varying combinations of drums, bass, electric guitar, saxophone, and the *frottoir*, which was played by his brother, Cleveland.

Chenier also played a dramatically broadened repertoire that drew on a then-fledgling genre known as rhythm and blues. From jukeboxes and radio, Chenier learned the infectious hits of artists including Fats Domino, Louis Jordan and His Tympani Five, Big Joe Turner, and B. B. King. With natural grace, he seamlessly adapted them to Creole French vocals and the piano accordion. It was a logical extension of his bursting talent and a quantum leap for Creole dance music. And just as this music began acquiring a new identity, thanks in large part to Clifton Chenier's efforts, its new name also was being formalized.

The phrase *"zaricots sont pas salés"* had been floating around for decades by this point — at least since 1934, and probably well before then — in a wide variety of songs such as "Je fait tout le tour du pays." Then, in 1949, blues guitarist Clarence Garlow recorded "Bon Ton Roula." Garlow lived in Beaumont, Texas, near the Louisiana border and well within the sphere of Creole culture. "Bon Ton Roula" was an R&B gem that combined an insistent, swirling rhumba rhythm with sensual horn arrangements and an eloquent guitar solo. But its most distinctive feature was the lyrics, which revealed the presence of an unknown subculture that functioned beneath the radar of mainstream America. By not bothering to contextualize the song for outsiders, Garlow made the implicit statement that most of his listeners were active participants in a thriving scene. The record was directed at people who would understand all of the references:

> You see me there, well, I ain't no fool,
> I'm one smart Frenchmen never been to
> school.
> Want to go somewhere in a Creole town,
> You stop and let me show you your way 'round
> And let the bon ton roula . . .
>
> At the church bazaar or the baseball game,
> At the French la-la, it's all the same
> You want to have fun now you got go
> Way out in the country to the zydeco.

Garlow sang the line about "zydeco" in dramatic a capella fashion, following a momentary break by the band.

The song's title came from the French *"bons temps rouler."* (Different spellings such as "Bon Ton Roulet" have been used by various record companies, and it appears on government copyright papers as "Bon Ton Rouleau.") The phrase *"laissez les bons temps rouler"* ("let the good times roll") appears often in zydeco and Cajun music. During the 1980s it was co-opted by the tourism industry as a symbol of Louisiana's joie de vivre, and eventually became quite clichéd. "Let the Good Times Roll" is also the title of several different rhythm and blues songs, one of which, by Louis Jordan, remains extemely popular both in zydeco and blues.

In this first public reference to "zydeco" as a separate entity, independent of the words *"sont pas salés,"* Garlow used it as a general term of celebration, with music as one key component. But soon zydeco came to refer specifically to music. It appeared with a wide variety of spellings that, like "Bon Ton Roula," were all phonetic attempts to spell French words in English. These efforts were complicated by the fact that Creole and Cajun French are primarily oral and aural traditions. Few French publications ever existed in southwestern Louisiana, as opposed to the many that once flourished in New Orleans, and formal frames of reference were limited. In addition, decades of isolation had left a legacy of low literacy. Thus while *"les haricots"* had become a popular term, its

multiple spellings during the 1950s included "zordico,""zologo," "zotticoe," and others. Some of these variants still appear occasionally.

The path to standardization was unintentionally blazed in Houston, Texas, where plentiful jobs have always attracted a lot of expatriate Creoles and Cajuns. They settled in ethnic enclaves such as the Fifth Ward neighborhood called Frenchtown. "That was a rough area," recalled progressive country artist Rodney Crowell, a Houston native. "I lived nearby, and I thought *we* were poor 'til I got a paper route over there when I was eleven." Frenchtown was a cohesive community, however, with plenty of places to go dancing, from Catholic church halls to nightclubs such as the Continental Zydeco Ballroom, Pe-Te's Cajun Barbecue, and the Silver Slipper. In addition, Frenchtown residents could easily commute to Louisiana for a weekend's infusion of fresh musical ideas. Clifton Chenier maintained a house in Houston, as well as one in Lafayette, and he proudly called both cities home.

Throughout the 1950s a Houston folklorist named Mack McCormick combed

Clifton Chenier and Chris Strachwitz of Arhoolie Records

the city's streets, taping and interviewing a diverse assortment of folk musicians. His collection was released in 1960 on a two-LP anthology entitled *A Treasury of Field Recordings.* The liner notes included McCormick's transcriptions of the lyrics to all of the songs. When he came to a bilingual version of the blues classic "Baby Please Don't Go" with the French phrase for snap beans, McCormick pondered awhile and then wrote it down as "zydeco."

"I agonized," McCormick told journalist Michael Tisserand years later. "My objective was to get as close to the sound of the thing as possible." Considering the pronunciation heard on most recordings from the 1930s on, McCormick did just that. To his surprise, "zydeco" soon became the norm on posters for Creole dances in Houston. In 1965, there was another pivotal moment when Clifton Chenier began a long relationship with Arhoolie Records. Its founder, Chris Strachwitz, went with McCormick's spelling, and since no one else in the record business was remotely interested in Creole music at the time, Arhoolie's zydeco albums set the global standard. The frugal Strachwitz did not promote his product with expensive ad campaigns or other trappings associated with major record labels. But through a network of aficionados he did get his albums distributed, broadcast, and reviewed around the world — and the world thought that "zydeco" worked just fine.

Most of the world did, anyway. Clifton Chenier recorded prolifically for Arhoolie and made his first trip to Europe in 1969, on an all-star package show called the American Folk and Blues Tour. This led to return engagements overseas and considerable acclaim among a devoted cult audience. The early-sixties blues revival, spurred by such British bands as the Rolling Stones and the Yardbirds, had created an adoring if somewhat naive atmosphere in Europe, where African-American blues musicians received far more respect, recognition, and money than they usually got at home.

As a unique stylist playing in peak form, Clifton Chenier quickly attained "living legend" status in Europe, and as such he was sought out by rock stars. According to one often-told story, perhaps a tall tale, Mick Jagger sent an intercessor to beg Chenier for a chance to sit in. Chenier had never heard of Jagger, much less of the Rolling Stones, and he sent back the contemptuous rebuff:

"*Nick?* That punk!" Chenier was also puzzled by the Europeans who often responded to his music with intense concentration but no dancing. "They just sat there like they was in a trance!" he recalled, shaking his head. Still, Chenier savored the memory of his audiences' obvious if immobile enjoyment.

Notoriously ornery in the business arena, Chenier did not have a savvy manager to put him on a career plane with such peers as B. B. King and Muddy Waters. But he did well for himself, and it is safe to assume that a debate on the correct spelling of "zydeco" would not have interested him in the least. Chenier was too busy creating the music, defining its modern sound, and winning new converts.

But others did debate it, in a dialogue that reflects the era's cultural upheaval. During the 1970s, southwest Louisiana was ablaze with linguistic activism fueled by fear that Cajun and Creole French were poised on the brink of extinction. Newly founded organizations such as CODOFIL, the Council for the Development of French in Louisiana, set up educational exchange programs with French-speaking nations around the world. In addition to its obvious resonance in France, this movement elicited an especially strong response in Quebec, where there was serious thought of secession from English-speaking Canada. Secession was never a real consideration in Louisiana, although Cajun rocker Zachary Richard, a pioneer in the cultural renaissance, refused for a time to answer anyone who addressed him in English.

More typically, many young people began an impassioned campaign on behalf of the region's language and heritage. This movement's leaders included Barry Ancelet, historian and linguist Ulysses Ricard, Jr., poet Debbie Clifton, musician and author Austin Sonnier, Michael Doucet, who went on to form the eclectic Cajun band BeauSoleil, and Nick Spitzer, Louisiana's first official state folklorist. They made contact with other French communities and treated zydeco and Cajun musicians with long-overdue respect.

One seminal event that embodied this new sentiment was the Tribute to Cajun Music, held in Lafayette in 1974. For the first time in Louisiana, zydeco and Cajun bands played in a formal concert setting with no dance floor, so that local people would focus on the cultural message of their music. The University of

Southwestern Louisiana supported the event and donated the use of the venue, an eight-thousand-seat arena. Folklorist Ralph Rinzler came down from the Smithsonian Institution to assist with production, lending the official imprimatur of his prestigious Washington employer. A legion of French journalists, brought to Louisiana by CODOFIL, was honored as the evening's special guests. Clifton Chenier graced the stellar lineup, which also included Bois-sec Ardoin and Canray Fontenot, Creole ballad singer Inez Catalon, Cajun fiddler and activist Dewey Balfa, twin fiddlers Dennis McGee and Sady Courville, and the bluesy Cajun accordionist Nathan Abshire, among others. The concert was a great success, and has become a highlight of the annual Festivals Acadien, held in Lafayette in mid-September.

Such official validation represented a radical change for Louisiana, where legislation passed in 1916 had forbidden children to speak French in the public schools. As a means of forcing assimilation, this law reinforced a worldview of disdain towards expressions of regional culture such as zydeco and Cajun music. The legislators thought that it would be best for Louisiana's French-speaking citizens to become ordinary, English-speaking Americans.

Zydeco and Cajun music had finally earned respect, but the debate over terminology continued. In 1984 the noted Québecois filmmaker André Gladu released a documentary on Creole dance music that was pointedly entitled *Zarico,* in recognition of the term's French roots. Gladu insisted that accuracy and cultural sensitivity made this the only acceptable spelling. Chris Strachwitz countered with the pragmatic observation that changing the name would confuse the public at the expense of working musicians and record sales. Meanwhile, Barry Ancelet made an intriguing connection that added substance to the discussion beyond intellectual turf wars.

While listening to some field recordings from the island of Rodrigue in the Indian Ocean, Ancelet heard the term *"zarico"* used in songs that were quite similar to *juré.* A closer look revealed many similarities between Rodrigue and south Louisiana. Both were agricultural enclaves where a black labor force descended from West African slaves had worked for a French ruling class. Both maintained a French-based dialect and a dance-music tradition centered around the accordion. On Rodrigue, *"zarico"* was used much as the phrase *"les haricots sont pas salés"* was used in Louisiana—as a term of general exclamation, without any specific context.

Such exuberance and joie de vivre in the context of dance music is always implicitly sexual, if not overtly so, as is dancing itself. Some *"zarico"* references on the Rodrigue recordings were far more blatant. One song, "Cari zarico," translates loosely as:

> I'm thinking what you're thinking, pretty girl.
> Hot bean soup.
> When the moon dances the sega, we'll
> harvest.
> Hot bean soup.

"When the moon dances the sega" refers to *"sega zarico,"* a tradition which unfolds on Rodrigue and several other islands nearby. This dance step mimics the planting of beans, as women move backwards, digging imaginary holes with their heels, closely followed by men who fill the holes with imaginary seed. In this setting, the beans—*"zarico"*—function as obvious symbols of courtship, sexuality, and fertility.

Ancelet suggested that the phrase's prevalence in Louisiana occurred for all of the same reasons. He supported this theory with sound research in linguistics and ethnomusicology. He observed that some uses in Louisiana—such as the popular refrain "let's zydeco all night long"—referred to courtship and sex, in addition to dancing. As a grassroots activist and a staunch supporter of working musicians, Ancelet did not insist that "zarico" should replace "zydeco" in common parlance. He also put linguistic preservation in perspective by recognizing that French had once been imposed upon much of Louisiana's black labor force, as had English.

Nick Spitzer conducted significant research as well, beginning in 1976 with extensive community-based fieldwork among rural Creole musicians. Spitzer uncovered another set of potential roots for the term "zydeco" in various West

African languages. In the Yula tongue, spoken north of the Ivory Coast, the words for "I dance" are *"a zaré."* In Ashanti, "I dance" is pronounced as either *"meré sa"* and *"meré go,"* while its Gurma equivalent is *"me dseré."* Spitzer also suggested that *"les haricots sont pas salés"* might be a deliberate pun created by Creole musicians who were aware of such West African phrases. The idea was not far-fetched, Spitzer argued, pointing out that the word "juke" — as in "juke joint" and "jukebox" — is generally believed to have derived from the pan-African word *"ndzugu,"* meaning "noise." As an active champion of working musicians, Spitzer, like Ancelet, did not support the implementation of "zarico."

Clifton Chenier stayed out of the theoretical arena but was a staunch linguistic supporter, nonetheless.

All my people speak French, and I learned it from them. A lot of people, they was kind of 'shamed of French, but one thing they didn't know was how important French is to 'em. You understand? You be around here, you meet a lot of people, they don't even know how to talk French, right here in Louisiana, but now, if they're in a city like Paris, they need it.

There's a lot of people holding back on French, you know, but me, I *never* was ashamed of French, and I never will be, because it go like this: if I can talk more than one language, I'm smarter than you! You can't speak but one language, and I got two or three of them I can talk, so who's the smartest?

If you go to Europe and you want to eat, the lady bring you the menu and now what you gonna tell her? You can't talk to her, you don't know what to order. Now I'm goin' to tell you this story. They had me, Earl Hooker, Magic Sam, Whistlin' Alex Moore, we all got on a plane in New York, and it took us nine hours to cross the ocean and get to Europe. [This was the previously mentioned tour in 1969.]

We got there, those boys from Chicago, Magic Sam and Earl Hooker, they laughed at me, said, "Oh, where y'all get that French from, can't you talk? You ain't nothin' but an old Frenchman." I ain't said nothin' to 'em.

So we got to France, we walk in a café. The lady asks me in French, "Can I help you, mister?" I told her, *"Oui, madame,* yes, ma'am'," you know. She said, "What do you want

to eat?" I say, *"Les oeufs, des grits, et du pain, "*that's grits, eggs, and toast bread. Okay, now, she got to them fellas, she asked them in French, they couldn't order nothin'. So I told her, I said, "Don't worry about them," I said, "I'm ordering their food." I told her in French. You know what I ordered them? A whole platter of raw fish! They eat that over there. I ordered Earl Hooker and them a whole platter of raw fish, and some pepper, and some salt, and some hard bread, hard as this brick here.

Chenier burst out laughing as he recalled his moment of sweet revenge.

I said, "Now eat that, all y'all so smart, now y'all eat that." They said, "No, man, we want what you got," and I said, "Well, then order it!" See, they couldn't do it, they had to eat some raw fish and, man, they wanted to kill me. And from that day on, all our tour in Europe, they never would tease me no more, 'cause they knew I had 'em there. Anything they wanted to drink, they had to ask in French, wanted some wine they had to order it in French. They had to depend on me, they followed me everywhere I go, man. I said, "Y'all gonna eat what I want y'all to eat."

There's probably some artistic license in Chenier's anecdote; few Parisian restaurants serve grits, except perhaps in Paris, Texas. But the story does reflect Chenier's pride in his heritage, years before such a stance became trendy. Nevertheless, Chenier was equally willing to sing in English or French and to adapt his repertoire to suit his audience. He explained, "We might go out tonight, and people don't want to hear nothin' but the blues. Go out tomorrow night, they don't want to hear nothin' but French music. Go somewhere else, they want to hear some hillbilly." (He pronounced this last word with emphasis on the second syllable.)

"We do all that," Chenier continued. "I like it all. It don't make me no difference. Whatever they ask for, if I know it, that's it, we play it. It makes me feel good if I make them feel good. That's what you're there for, not to satisfy you, satisfy the people."

In an effort to satisfy the people—and to score a lucrative hit in the process—Chenier approached recording in a similarly eclectic way. In 1954 he started out on a small, black-owned label called Elko Records, cutting seven songs at a radio station in Lake Charles, Louisiana. This was a common practice at the time, when

recording studios as such were less prevalent than they are today. Some of this debut material was slow blues, sung in English, while songs such as "Louisiana Stomp" were up-tempo romps that captured Chenier's fresh approach to zydeco and his command of the piano accordion. None of the material was wildly original—Chenier would never be known as a prolific songwriter—but all of it was spirited. The Elko material was leased to Imperial Records, a major

label that featured such rhythm and blues stars as Fats Domino, and Chenier's name began to circulate nationally.

The next move by Elko's owner, J. R. Fulbright, was to unselfishly introduce his young artist to another prominent national company, Specialty Records. At the time, musicians on Specialty's successful R&B roster ranged from the frantic Little Richard to the suave crooner Percy Mayfield. In 1955 Chenier went to Specialty's studio in Los Angeles to work with famed producer Bumps Blackwell.

"Clifton's band was traveling around in an old station wagon," Blackwell told journalist Greg Drust. "When I got them in the studio I pulled half of the guys out. I didn't let that many of them play. It kind of upset them, because they had their own little thing going, but me, I knew what was going to work on the record. I wanted to get that accordion out front."

As befits a producer whose credits included Little Richard's "Tutti Frutti" and Sam Cooke's "You Send Me," Blackwell's instincts were on target. The Specialty sessions yielded some great material, including a raucous shuffle with a French vocal entitled "Ay-tete-fee." This was Specialty's attempt at a phonetic spelling of *"eh, petite fille"*—"hey, little girl"; on reissue albums, years later, they finally got it right. Other notable songs included the zydeco instrumentals

Philip Walker, one of Clifton Chenier's early guitarists

"Boppin' the Rock" and "Squeeze Box Boogie." The latter became a jukebox favorite in Jamaica.

None of these records were successful in America, however, and neither were Chenier's efforts at mainstream rhythm and blues, sung in English. They did sell well enough to put Chenier and his band on the national touring circuit of R&B clubs and concert halls, including a cameo appearance at New York's famed Apollo Theater. For several years during the late 1950s, Clifton Chenier traveled around the nation, playing rhythm and blues and zydeco on his accordion and singing in both French and English. He crossed the paths of such stars as Ray Charles, Little Richard, and Chuck Berry, and worked alongside a virtual

"who's who" of blues, R&B, and rock artists, including singers Bobby "Blue" Bland, Junior Parker, and Jimmy McCracklin, guitarists T-Bone Walker and Pee Wee Crayton, and organist Bill Doggett, of "Honky Tonk" fame. Singer Etta James toured with Chenier, and since she was still under age, Chenier became her chaperon—no easy job, because she had eyes for one of his musicians. A close call with a different type of trouble came when police in Mississippi thought that the light-skinned minor James was white. Fortunately James had legal documents that proved otherwise.

To help Chenier polish his act and improve his English stage patter, booking agent Howard Lewis hooked him up with blues guitarist Lowell Fulson. Fulson's 1950s hits included "Reconsider, Baby" and "Black Nights," and the 1967 classic "Tramp." He toured with Chenier as the band's special guest, and coached him on how to dress, speak, and act like a pro. "Cliff was a country boy," Fulson told Michael Tisserand, "so you could always find something for him to tidy up a little bit . . . I showed him about all he needed, and then after about a year I got hung up with another band. But I hated to leave them old boys." Chenier, for his part, was always quick to acknowledge Fulson's help. "He'd talk to me and I'd listen," he told Ann Allen Savoy.

Fulson's "Reconsider, Baby" had appeared on Chess Records, and in 1956 the prestigious Chicago label signed Chenier to its Checker subsidiary. This made him a colleague of such blues titans as Muddy Waters, Howlin' Wolf, and Little Walter, but Chenier's most notable recording for Checker was a slice of contemporary R&B entitled "My Soul." It was the most commercially conscious song that Chenier ever cut, replete with backup vocalists who sang doo-wop harmony triplets. Although it was a powerful number that remained a staple on Chenier's live shows, "My Soul" did not catch on, and Chenier's tenure with Checker was short-lived.

Chenier continued touring, hiring a succession of young guitarists who would later lead their own successful blues bands. Lonnie Brooks, Philip Walker, and Lonesome Sundown all speak highly of Chenier as a bandleader and teacher, though they are quick to add that he was strict. During the seventies such prominent players as accordionist Stanley "Buckwheat" Dural and guitarist Sonny Landreth also benefitted from Chenier's tutelage, and then went on to successful solo careers. But by the late fifties, Chenier's own career was dead slow. His next move was several notches down, in the form of three sessions for Zynn Records, one of the many small labels run by Jay Miller in Crowley, Louisiana.

Miller was a paradoxical figure, even by the generous standards of the south Louisiana music milieu. Reviled for a vicious series of white-supremacist "party" records such as "Nigger Hating Me," Miller showed a completely contradictory side in his flair for producing soulful and evocative blues records by black artists. Miller would score a huge hit in 1966 with "Baby, Scratch My Back" by Baton Rouge harmonicist Slim Harpo. Improbably, this swamp-blues classic went way past the logical confines of southern black radio, and climbed the national charts at white Top 40 stations. Jay Miller did a typically good job of producing Clifton Chenier on sessions in 1958, 1959, and 1960. He brought in Katie Webster, the great south Louisiana session pianist, who added a complementary keyboard texture behind Chenier's accordion. Saxophonist Lionel Prevost wailed in wild sympathetic abandon. But once again, these records went nowhere.

The early 1960s found Clifton Chenier working the Gulf Coast "crawfish circuit" between New Orleans and Houston and languishing without a record deal. Fortunately, he had an ally and advocate in his cousin by marriage, the great Texas blues guitarist Lightnin' Hopkins. One night in 1964 Hopkins brought Chris Strachwitz to hear Chenier at a little beer joint near the Houston Ship Channel. Strachwitz recalled the evening in an interview with Ted Fox, a music journalist who went on to manage Chenier protégé Stanley "Buckwheat" Dural.

> Lightnin' asked me, "Chris, do you want to go see my cuz?" I said, "Who's your cousin?" He said, "Cliff, Clifton Chenier." The name rang a bell because I think I had a Specialty record by him, and maybe a Checker. To me that was rhythm and blues. I wasn't all that enthusiastic, but if Lightnin' wanted to go there — I was just like his little dog. I said, "Sure, let's go over and see him." So we went over to Frenchtown in Houston. I'll never forget. We walked into one of those little beer joints — hardly anybody in it, there was two couples dancing. There was this man with this accordion and just a drummer. He didn't have no band at all. He was playing these really low-down blues. Mostly in French, but some in English, too. Clifton came up to me afterwards and said, "Oh, you making records? Come on, make me one!"

The two hit it off. They struck a deal, arranged a recording session for the very next day, and converged at Houston's Gold Star studio. Over the years, numerous record companies had used this facility for sessions by such important regional stylists as Cajun/western swing fiddler Harry Choates and country singer George Jones.

Strachwitz was dismayed when Chenier arrived at Gold Star with a full band. As Bumps Blackwell had done ten years before, Strachwitz wanted to emphasize Chenier's impressive accordion work. Quite unlike Blackwell, however, Strachwitz was motivated by a purist aesthetic, and he recoiled at making any concessions in order to craft a hit. He wanted Chenier to record traditional Creole music, in French, with minimal instrumentation. Chenier was convinced that his best shot at success was something in a Ray Charles vein — rhythm and blues, with a full band, sung in English. Equally opinionated and adamant, Strachwitz and Chenier eventually found middle ground by recording songs in both styles, with a wide variety in between.

From the first session at Gold Star, Strachwitz released a single entitled "Ay Ai Ai." It inspired some hometown sales and spins on local jukeboxes, and helped Chenier get better bookings in Texas and Louisiana. But Arhoolie was not equipped for the aggressive promotion required to turn a "single" into a national hit. Besides the legitimate costs involved, such campaigns could include a hefty budget for payola. Strachwitz had no desire to compete in that arena. His vision, rather, was to document the music — old-fashioned, folkloric, or downright strange — that hit-oriented labels wouldn't touch. "I never looked at it as a business," Strachwitz told Ted Fox. "I only recorded something because I liked it. If I even *thought* it had commercial potential, I'd probably reject it."

Strachwitz released more singles by Clifton Chenier during the next few years, but they were mainly manufactured for jukeboxes and radio stations on the Gulf Coast circuit. When these songs were packaged on LPs in the late 1960s sales were much better, thanks to an overlapping following among the "hippie" counterculture and hardcore blues fans, in both America and Europe. Despite Strachwitz's stated aversion to commercial potential, Chenier was Arhoolie's highest-selling artist, and it was for Arhoolie that he recorded his finest work, on albums considered among the best in all of zydeco. These include *Louisiana Blues and Zydeco, Live at Montreux,* and *Bogalusa Boogie.* By the time they appeared, Chenier had named his group the Red Hot Louisiana Band.

Chenier's success encouraged Strachwitz to pursue zydeco and Cajun music in greater depth. Arhoolie has an extensive and eclectic catalogue, but it is in south Louisiana that Strachwitz has made his most important and lasting mark, by documenting the scene and bringing national exposure to the music community. The cultural renaissance that began in the late 1970s owes much to his work from the previous decade.

That renaissance was also presaged by Clifton Chenier's performances at

Clifton Chenier and the Red Hot Louisiana Band at the New Orleans Jazz & Heritage Festival

white venues in the late 1960s. At the time this was a groundbreaking occurrence. One of the most popular spots informally integrated by Chenier was Jay's Lounge and Cockpit in the small town of Cankton, near Lafayette. Chenier was also one of the first French-singing, Creole or Cajun musicians to cross over to a young, educated, urban audience—not that Jay's was a swanky bistro. The crowd was evenly divided between people wearing sandals and those sporting cowboy boots, and the "Cockpit" part of the name referred to a staging area for cockfights, which are still legal in Louisiana. "The rooster who didn't survive was usually served to the band in a 'loser's gumbo,'" Michael Doucet recalled.

"Lots of great musicians played at Jay's," Barry Ancelet said. "Asleep at the Wheel, the Fabulous Thunderbirds, Marcia Ball, Edgar Winter and White Trash. But Clifton Chenier was the first zydeco bandleader to work there. His music was incredible. He would pack the place and play for hours on end, and we would all dance 'til we were exhausted." Michael Doucet observed that "Clifton opened the doors for all the young, Cajun counterculture groups that followed. A lot of us played at Jay's and we loved it—bands like Rufus Jagneaux, Red Beans and Rice, and two bands of mine—Coteau, and then BeauSoleil." When Jay's closed down around 1980, some of these groups began playing at a zydeco dance hall called Hamilton's. Situated on what was then the outskirts of Lafayette, Hamilton's is now an atmospheric anachronism in the midst of suburban sprawl. The occasional evenings when zydeco bands are not featured are still referred to as "white night."

By the 1980s, hard living and constant travel had ravaged Clifton Chenier's health. He laid low for a few years, and underwent major surgery. Doctors and family members advised Chenier to quit touring; he was in his mid-fifties, and needed to slow down. But Chenier's determined response was "die over here or die on the bandstand," as his guitarist Paul "Little Buck" Senegal told Michael Tisserand. Chenier set up a complicated and arduous schedule of national travel and on-the-road dialysis treatments. The twice-weekly intravenous procedure kept Chenier alive but weakened his arms, so he began playing a specially designed lightweight accordion and squeezing rubber balls to tone his muscles. I was lucky enough to see Chenier often in those days, at the Blue Angel and the Grant Street Dance Hall in Lafayette, the Casino Club in St. Martinville, and various clubs in New Orleans. Some nights he was vibrant, while at other times he seemed to be at death's door — all depending, the band told me, on how much time had passed since his last dialysis session.

Either way, Chenier insisted on playing a single set of three or four hours' length, with no breaks.

People ask me how I can get up on the bandstand and play four hours without stopping. It's because I've always been a hard worker, *always*. When I get up there, I'm *up there*, no half-steppin'. And when I tell you "goodnight" you can hand me a thousand dollars and I ain't gonna play no more. Not when I say "goodnight," that's it.

We give the people they money's worth, and a lot of people they enjoying themself. Man, *I* enjoy that. A lot of old people come to my dance, they be havin' a stick, and when they leave the dance they can't find the stick no more. I say, *"Quoi qu'arrivait avec ton baton?"* ("What happened to your stick?"), and they say, *"Oh, j'ai pas de baton, je l'ai jeté dehors!"* In other words, they ain't got no more stick, they throwed it outside 'cause they didn't need it no more!

In 1984 Clifton Chenier received one of his highest career honors—a Grammy award for *I'm Here!*, as the best traditional or ethnic recording released in 1983.

Although Chenier remained on good terms with Chris Strachwitz, the album appeared on Alligator Records, a Chicago label that took a far more aggressive approach to promotion and marketing than Arhoolie. "When I got with the right record company, they pushed it," Chenier told Barry Ancelet. *I'm Here!* was not Chenier's best album, but, as he observed, "That award is for a whole career, partner. You got to earn it. I figure that French music suit me, and I stuck with it. That's what got me that Grammy. And I'll tell you something, when you go to the Grammys, you see more diamonds than you ever saw in your life." Appropriately, Chenier acknowledged his royal status on the album's opening track, "Let's Do the Zydeco": "They call me the king, the king of Zydeco..."

The award gave Chenier an emotional boost during his last years, and issued a defiant response to people who had written him off. Sadly, this group included several of his zydeco-accordionist colleagues. As Chenier's strength dwindled, they hovered none too subtly, waiting for the king to expire. After ending a northeastern tour at New York's Lone Star Cafe, Chenier returned to Lafayette and passed away days later, on December 12, 1987. Many former bandmembers attended Chenier's wake in Opelousas, including several whom he had fired en masse amidst the stress of the decline that he had fought so tenaciously. Chenier's funeral was held the next day, in Lafayette. As is often the case at such rites for prominent musicians, Chenier's brilliant career was barely mentioned. The generic eulogy focused instead on his chances for redemption. In a more personalized and respectful vein, his son C. J. played "I'm Coming Home," a secular song that Clifton had written for his mother. The poignant number also works well as a spiritual, and it certainly did so that day, in a church packed well past capacity.

Just three weeks later, the zydeco pretenders began vying for Chenier's crown. The crown was a tangible object, as well as an abstract concept; since 1971 Chenier had sported an elaborate piece of regal headwear that, he told me, he had won at an accordion contest in Europe. Like the story about the grits in Paris, this anecdote had an apocryphal edge. Chenier might well have been inspired by the penchant for "monarchy merchandising" in the Lafayette business community, as demonstrated by "the king of seafood" and "the king of

Hiram Sampy at home after a Saturday barbeque

mobile homes," who appeared on local television with their crowns prominently displayed. Perhaps this trend was a literal interpretation of Huey Long's egalitarian pronouncement "Every man a king." One fact was indisputable, however. "I'll tell you what," Chenier said, "to take that crown away they'd have to roll me." But Chenier had the confidence and ability to look natural in this getup, as opposed to the "clown princes" who donned crowns at their own self-appointed coronations.

Rockin' Dopsie, in particular, tarnished his long-standing good name with one evening's ill-conceived decision to stage his own investiture in Lafayette, in January of 1988. Dopsie then made matters worse with a ludicrous story about Chenier passing him both the crown and zydeco's torch from his death bed. Unfortunately this tale was picked up by the media, is still repeated, and has acquired some credibility. But Dopsie was more naive than malevolent, and he never understood why so many people were offended. Stanley "Buckwheat" Dural dismissed the coronation as "crude," while Chenier's trumpeter, Warren Ceasar, said, "Dopsie could have waited. This looks like he was just waiting for Clifton to pass on." Although Dopsie was roasted in the local press as an opportunist, Barry Ancelet offered a different view: "Lots of people took that the wrong way, and Dopsie was shocked and hurt. He was a decent man. I believe that his intention was to provide some stability and healing for a musical community that was in mourning."

Rockin' Dopsie (pronounced DOOP-see) had emerged on the zydeco scene not long after Chenier, and then spent the next quarter-century in his shadow. Perhaps he felt that this was his time, after years of paying dues and playing "second accordion." With Chenier gone, Dopsie was zydeco's best-known bandleader for the moment, although others would soon surge past him. To fuel this regal fantasy, Dopsie had already hired several of Chenier's ex-musicians to join his band, the Cajun Twisters. (The band featured Rockin' Dopsie, Jr., on *frottoir* and vocals; after Rockin' Dopsie's death in 1993, Jr. took over the group and now bills himself as "Rockin' Dopsie," creating some confusion.)

Beyond making his own prolific recordings, Rockin' Dopsie, Sr., played an important role in popularizing zydeco when he appeared on Paul Simon's *Graceland*. Dopsie and the Cajun Twisters backed the singer-songwriter on "That Was Your Mother," an up-tempo tune that paired Simon's lyrics with zydeco accompaniment based on the traditional song "Josephine est pas ma femme." The critically acclaimed *Graceland* was Paul Simon's best-selling album, and received the prestigious Album of the Year Award at the 1987 Grammys. Rockin' Dopsie responded by threatening to sue Simon for the publishing and broadcast revenues from "That Was Your Mother," which Simon had registered as an original composition. When the archaic folk roots of its melody could not be traced to any specific songwriter, Dopsie abandoned the case.

Graceland did bring Rockin' Dopsie recognition, as well as a short-lived contract with corporate giant Atlantic Records. But Paul Simon had hired Dopsie only because Clifton Chenier was unavailable due to illness, and it was Chenier whom Simon mentioned in the lyrics of "That Was Your Mother." Only Clifton Chenier could wear zydeco's crown with regal grace, back it up with regal talent, and look like a natural-born king.

Chenier's legacy resonates in many ways. Most obviously, his son C. J. maintains the family tradition with prolific touring and recording. Stanley "Buckwheat" Dural, who gave up mainstream R&B to work with Chenier, has emerged as the genre's most successful and influential artist, performing under the stage name Buckwheat Zydeco. Younger players such as Nathan Williams and Geno Delafose have embraced Chenier's ideas and the piano accordion while developing their own styles and original material. Accordionists Jude Taylor, Hiram Sampy, Leon Sam, T. Black, Al Rapone, Fernest Arceneaux, Sunpie Barnes, Zydeco Joe, and Roy Carrier base their music more directly on Chenier's repertoire. Carrier owns a zydeco dance hall, the Offshore Lounge, in Lawtell, Louisiana, where he encourages young, entry-level players to hone their skills at weekly jam sessions. Successful graduates of this informal school include Roy's son Chubby, a sophisticated modernist. And Roy Carrier is a zydeco torch bearer himself, as a student and cousin of such la-la artists as Bébé, Eraste, and Calvin Carrière. As Chenier observed, "Lotta youngsters don't want to hear about zydeco music, but they got to remember one thing:

their daddy been born and raised on that. All them youngsters should follow their daddy's footsteps sometime."

Chenier's influence also persists on broader levels. The emergence and growth of the New Orleans Jazz & Heritage Festival and the Southwest Louisiana Zydeco Festival were immeasurably enhanced by his participation. Both events have helped bring zydeco to its current level of popularity. There are many important figures on the contemporary zydeco scene that Clifton Chenier bequeathed to the world in such promising condition, and their stories follow. Since Rockin' Dopsie's postfuneral follies, none has made a serious claim to zydeco's throne. But they all acknowledge that zydeco does have a reigning elder statesman: Wilson "Boozoo" Chavis.

The World of Rural Zydeco

**Boozoo Chavis:
Creole Cowboy**

They got all these guys out here playin' one thing and sayin' something else," Boozoo Chavis snorted with contempt. It was an appropriately feisty beginning to a lengthy and indignant interview, conducted in Chavis's front yard in 1987. "They're sayin' 'zydeco, zydeco,'" Chavis continued, leaning forward in his lawn chair and wagging his index finger. "But them jokers ain't no more playin' zydeco than I'm jumpin' out the window! I want to show the world what zydeco is." These were strong words, but Wilson "Boozoo" Chavis (pronounced CHAY-viss) continues to back them up with more than half a century's zydeco credentials. Born in 1928, Chavis began playing zydeco dances back in the late 1940s. In 1954 he recorded zydeco's first popular single, "Paper in My Shoe," eclipsing Clifton Chenier for that distinction.

Chavis does not believe that he received anything close to a fair share of the record's profits, and additional dealings reinforced his sense that people were "getting funny with the money." In the early 1960s Chavis withdrew from the music business in disgust. Turning to another skilled trade, he spent the next twenty years training racehorses and raising his family. In his fifties, older and wiser, Chavis decided to give music a second chance. He resumed playing dances in 1984 and has been packing in crowds ever since all along the crawfish circuit. Chavis's dances in Louisiana and Texas are booked solid far in advance, in between his forays around the continent. These gatherings also reveal Chavis as a master merchandiser who sells souvenir briefs and panties that are embossed with two-part instructions: "Take 'em off! Throw 'em in the corner!"

At age seventy, Chavis is a generation older than most other zydeco bandleaders, and is treated with considerable respect. While not the new "king" of zydeco, he is certainly regarded as a father figure. Since his comeback, Chavis has inspired a host of young admirers and imitators, and has started some of zydeco's silliest yet most entertaining trends. In 1986 Chavis's "Dog Hill" created a craze for zydeco songs with canine themes, complete with barking. Three years later, "Zydeco Hee Haw" lent similar celebrity status to songs about mules and singers who could imitate them. Chavis is even the subject of an amorous tribute—"Old Man's Sweetheart"—that scored a regional hit for a newly emerging singer named Donna Angelle. "I want a man like Boozoo...," Angelle's breathy fantasy begins.

Adulation, a hectic schedule, and the resulting lack of privacy have made Chavis view his late-blooming success with mixed emotions: "It spring up just like that, and sometimes I tell people, I say, 'I'm scared of myself.' Yessir. It's true. You get scared of yourself. And I'm not afraid nobody gonna do me nothing, nobody gonna kill me or nothing like that, but I'm just afraid, you know? It's too much. It do you funny. I could have bought me a Cadillac, but I don't need it. I don't try to act proud, I'm still me. Some of them guys, they want to change into five different color suits every night. I don't need all that." Even when Chavis was given a zydeco crown, in a matter of minutes he replaced it with his cowboy hat.

Boozoo Chavis does not approach Clifton Chenier's prowess or versatile ability to "zydeco-ize" commercial R&B material. Chavis makes no such claim because he clearly understands the reason for his popularity. "I'm not bragging for myself," he explained, "but this style of music what I got, it's gonna make you dance. It's definitely gonna make you dance." Chavis's music, played on a diatonic accordion, is raw, raucous, and rural — a deeply Afro-Caribbean form of zydeco that owes little to outside influences, except the blues. It is shamelessly repetitious; once a lyrical or melodic idea is introduced, further development is virtually nil. The only line in "Dog Hill," for instance — "I'm going to Dog Hill, where the pretty women at!" — is continually restated over an accordion riff that's too simplistic to be considered a melody, and which has no chord changes or harmonic resolution. Such minimalism is never dull, however, because what Boozoo Chavis lacks in complexity is counterbalanced by his ferocious, irresistible groove.

In a time-honored folk tradition, Chavis plays with idiosyncratic disregard for conventional musical structure. He tends to "jump time" by changing chords at random or dropping and adding beats so that 2-and-4 become 1-and-3, or some even stranger fraction. Chavis makes no apologies for his quirks and caprices.

You know I have my sons in my band, and sometimes they say, "You ought to practice, when we gonna practice?" And I say, "I ain't practicin', me. Y'all practice." They want to change me to their style, they want me to count "one, two, three," and I tell 'em, "You

Boozoo Chavis in his stable at Dog Hill

can't break me, I got my habit. In forty years ain't no one break me yet." Sometimes they say, "Boozoo, you out of time!" My youngest boy, the drummer, he'll say, "Daddy, watch your beat, you jumpin' time," and I tell him, "Don't tell me to watch my beat, you watch me. If it's wrong, do it wrong, with me! If I'm wrong, you wrong, too!"

Some people say, "Boozoo, boy, you play a number that I'd sure like to play," they say, "You gonna show me how to play, I'm gonna go to your house and learn to play the accordion," all that, but they can't catch it. My fingers work fast, up and down, just like a typewriting machine. Yessir. And if I hear a song I like, and I say, "I can play that," then I'll catch it, and then I'll change it a little bit, to my style.

Not surprisingly, Chavis has little patience for modern recording sessions and their attendant high-tech demands. He is famous for cutting entire albums in three hours without stopping, just as he plays a dance. Such sessions have an overrated reputation for capturing authentic, spontaneous performances. Spark and spirit are more important than pristine audio engineering, of course, but most albums produced under these rushed circumstances — all too common in zydeco — are poorly recorded, to the artist's ultimate detriment. In 1991 producer Terry Adams of the rock band NRBQ prevailed on Chavis to record under more conventional conditions, including a thorough "setup" to properly position all the microphones and check the sound levels that were going onto tape. The result was one of his better albums, simply entitled *Boozoo Chavis,* on the Elektra-Nonesuch American Explorer Series. This was Chavis's first album to receive significant national attention, which led to media adulation, higher performance fees, and appearances at prestigious venues. Still, Chavis did not enjoy the experience.

"They strain me when I'm in the studio," he complained. "They put that earphone on me. My head is flat, and that thing go to slipping and sliding. You playing, and then after awhile that thing slip back, and the man, the engineer, he say, 'You need an adjustment.' That's why I don't like them earphones when I go in that studio. Shit. I can hear the music, I don't need that. I know where I'm at."

Chavis started learning "where he was at" as a young boy, during the 1930s. His rough-hewn approach harkens back to the pre-zydeco "la-la" era. Chavis was raised in a semirural section of Lake Charles known as Dog Hill, where music was very much a homegrown, informal affair centered around his father's accordion.

In them days when we were small, Mama would carry us everywhere they would go. We had a wagon and horses. They'd go to those old house dances, and leave us sleeping in the wagon outside. We'd hear the music comin' through the windows.

When I got a little bigger, I would sit inside and watch, and Daddy'd let me scratch a little on the rubboard. Then when he put the accordion down to take a break, I'd grab it and play, and he'd say, "Oh, you gonna learn, you." He played every weekend. I learned by watching him. I was nine years old. He'd work his fingers slow and tell me, "Do like this, do like that, push and pull." I did that, and I kept on.

When I got older I learned from some other guys—Leonard Pitre, Joseph Jackson, Tee Ma Guidry, Ray Sam—and I started playin' family dances. See, I was ridin' horses on a bush track, and I won a race. I took the money and bought a heifer. Then I sold the heifer, and bought an accordion for thirty-five dollars.

When I got married in 1952 I was playing dances for my uncle and all of them, family dances. They had them house dances and they say, "How 'bout you come play next Sunday," and all that. Okay, I'd go play over there, play accordion. And sometimes we didn't have no rubboard, sometimes they had things what you scrub clothes with, with the wooden legs on them. Washboard. Well, they used to play that with a spoon. Scratch, scratch, scratch, scratch, they did it like that, just for a beat. And when I started playing I used to keep the beat with my foot. I played sitting down. Now I play standing up. It looks better. But a long time ago them old people, they played the accordion sitting down, so I did, too. And they'd give us five dollars, ten dollars, that was good money at the time.

Every little bit helped, Chavis observed:

Times were hard when we grew up. We used to have to walk five miles to get to school. And we'd go to school, we'd bring some corn bread and cocoa for lunch, corn bread and egg, biscuit and egg. Bologna, we didn't know what that was. Shit. We had red beans and corn bread. When the teacher would ring the bell, we'd go out there to eat, sometimes we'd be ashamed to get our lunch out of our bag. Them other children come from town, they had some good lunch meat and apples and oranges. You ashamed to come out with corn bread in front of them children.

We'd go to school and sometimes we didn't have no socks. In the wintertime we'd put paper in our shoes to warm our feet, that's the God's truth. That's where that song "Paper in My Shoe" comes from. Kids today are blessed.

Chavis's "Paper in My Shoe" does not elaborate on the subject of tough times; it merely repeats the phrase without comment or thematic development. The image appears in other songs, however, such as "What My Mama Told Me," by the late Chicago blues artist Junior Wells: "Somebody asked me, what does a poor boy do? / He sews patches on his clothes, and stuffs newspaper in his shoe."

"Yeah, times were hard when we came up," Chavis recalled. "But I kept playing at house parties and dances. Lots of people in my family had these little clubs, and I played at all of 'em. The Club Continental, Club 15, Club 16. Clifton Chenier played at some of 'em, too, he lived around here. I played at all of them places, and I got better and better."

Word of Chavis's talent started to spread, and caught the attention of Goldband Records and its subsidiary label, Folk-Star. Owned by Eddie Shuler, Goldband had already recorded the brilliant Cajun accordionist and singer, Iry LeJeune, and went on to document a rich variety of south Louisiana swamp pop and blues artists, such as Cookie and the Cupcakes, Hop Wilson, and

Boozoo and Poncho Chavis at Richard's Club

Cleveland Crochet, of "Sugar Bee" fame. Few of these venerable musicians had positive memories about working with or recording for the company. "It's just like you getting me to do this interview today," Chavis said, "and then the day gonna come when this interview gonna be worthwhile for you. I didn't know nothing about business or royalties. But I goes in the studio, and they start counting off the time, and they say, 'Hold it, you come in too slow. Try it again,' all that. We went in there at six o'clock that evening, we come out of there two-thirty that morning. It took that long."

Despite such effort, "Paper in My Shoe" was not a very good record. Chavis was jumping time wildly, and the studio musicians didn't know how to jump with him. A strong groove would have lent some charm to the chaos, but that was missing, too, since Boozoo's unorthodox technique left everyone musically mystified. To further complicate matters, the band members were woefully out of tune, both with each other and with Chavis's accordion. Nevertheless, "Paper in My Shoe" was eventually leased to Imperial Records. Eddie Shuler has stated that it sold over a hundred thousand copies. Boozoo Chavis certainly believed this set of sales figures, and he assumed that a decent share of that money would be his. "And when I be telling you this, I'm mad now," he fumed. "If they came from Goldband today and asked me to make another record, I believe I'd have to shoot 'em. You can go to Goldband right now and look upstairs. He kept Iry LeJeune's records, and he's putting them out now that Iry LeJeune is dead. Been dead over thirty years, but they're coming out with his records. When I'm dying, he gonna come out with mine."

Chavis is one of many Creole and Cajun musicians whose encounters with the recording industry left them embittered. Exploitation and shady dealings continue to victimize black and white artists alike. But Chavis's story also reveals an ugly legacy of the racism that he first experienced as a child and encountered again in the wake of his first record.

Sometimes I'd go to town with my mama when I was little, and people would say in French, *"Gardez ce 'tit nègre,"* you know, "Look at that little nigger," that's what they'd call me. And boy, it'd make me mad. I didn't say nothing. They didn't think I could talk French. And I'd just keep going, but that make you ashamed.

But it don't worry me now, now that I'm makin' money playing music. Now I say 'piss on them,' excuse my language. Now it speak as good as it don't speak. I don't care. And I walk in them stores and they respect me now. Yessir. You know when I came up, there was a lot of Uncle Toms. But now I don't give a damn. I walk in them stores now, I say, "Give me this, give me that," I pull out my checkbook. I get in them stores, and they say, "Hey, Boozoo, how you doin'?" And the man don't want to shake hands with me, but I make him shake hands. I say, "How you doin'?," yeah. I don't care about them . . . they all prejudiced in there. But I been knowing them so long now, they respect me.

Chavis's comments underscore the hardly surprising point that racism still affects the zydeco scene — no more so than it does in any other social milieu, perhaps, but certainly no less. One glaring manifestation is the fact that white people are generally welcome at zydeco dance halls, but black people are quite unwelcome at most Cajun nightspots, except the few that cater to tourists. Some rural Cajun dancehalls reluctantly let black people in, albeit with a cool reception. Others have tried to deny them admission by claiming private club status. In one instance such a spurious attempt sparked federal civil rights litigation and a lot of harsh publicity. As part of the settlement, the club had to prominently post a sign stating that nobody would be turned away.

Alphonse "Bois-sec" Ardoin (center) with Dirk Powell and Christine Balfa of Balfa Toujours

There have also been threats of cancellation and violence when black musicians sit in with Cajun bands at white clubs or even when they are simply asked to do so. In 1997 zydeco accordionist Geno Delafose was invited to play with guitarist Christine Balfa, in the small town of Basile. Controversy and threats ensued, but Balfa, a daughter of the late Cajun fiddler Dewey Balfa and leader of the band Balfa Toujours, courageously stood her ground, and Delafose played. Balfa articulately explained her position in a letter to the local newspaper: "I can tell you, a large part of what we consider Cajun music came from the influence of the Creoles. It is something we should be proud of."

The rich legacy of Cajun-Creole collaboration dates back to the 1920s, when a talented white fiddler named Dennis McGee recorded with Amédé Ardoin. But Ardoin's career was allegedly ended by racial violence, when he was beaten for accepting a white woman's handkerchief to wipe his brow. Ardoin survived the attack but lost his faculties. Racial interchanges have continued over the years, however, including Clifton Chenier's recordings with swamp pop crooner Rod Bernard in 1976 and Michael Doucet's appearance with zydeco accordionist Nathan Williams on the album *Creole Crossroads* in 1995. Everyone involved has benefitted, but some people feel threatened by such interaction.

Some racial hostility in zydeco and Cajun music circles is generated by black people. Although zydeco club owners encourage everyone to come out and dance, black women may accuse white women of "trying to steal our men." Disparaging remarks towards whites in general are also heard on occasion. But the crucial difference between these incidents and those described above is that such attitudes are purely personal. They do not reflect the policy of the clubs' management, and are not encouraged; if nothing else, white patrons are good for business. Overall, most zydeco dance halls boast a very friendly atmosphere, and are extremely hospitable places. Efficient security is maintained in the unlikely event that problems of any kind do arise.

Tension still exists, too, between light- and dark-skinned blacks. "I used to play at the Triangle Club in Frilot Cove," accordionist Jeffery Broussard told Michael Tisserand. "It was a real nice place, real huge. It would stay packed just about every weekend. There was only one thing that was different about it, and excuse me for saying this, but I felt that it was wrong . . . it was like all the blacks were on the left-hand side, and the lighter people — they called themselves mulatto — were on the right-hand side." Broussard asserted that the issue was solved at the Triangle Club when "the young generation blew that out of the water" by simply refusing to accept such bias. But these problems persist, and are still reported by other musicians.

Boozoo Chavis is sensitive to the nuances of prejudice, and the anecdote that he resents the most surrounds the recording of "Paper in My Shoe" in 1954. It is alleged that Chavis got drunk during the session, fell off his chair, and recorded zydeco's first hit while lying flat on his back. Chavis's disgust with the story is fueled in part by its condescension and implicit racial stereotyping. "Shit! How the hell you gonna keep playing like that?" he asked with rhetorical rage. "They made that up."

Eddie Shuler's patronizing version of the event has appeared often in print — he once referred to Chavis as "a natural-born clown" — and thus achieved some credibility. Shuler professed surprise at Chavis's reaction, and told Michael Tisserand that "Boozoo always denied falling off that stool, but that's the best commercial he could ever have. You couldn't even dream up something that valuable. But he doesn't look at it like that."

Against his better judgment, Chavis did record for Eddie Shuler again in 1960, and was disappointed with the results, which did not yield a promising single. As on "Paper in My Shoe," the musicians were out of tune and out of time with each other. The only memorable moment was provided by the sheer oddity of a selection entitled "Hamburgers and Popcorn," which left Chavis feeling nauseated with Goldband Records and the larger entity of the music industry. "I got disgusted," he said, "and I just stopped playing. I was training horses and running at a bunch of different tracks in Louisiana and Texas. I did that for many years. Then I came back to music in 1984 and cut "Dog Hill" for Floyd Soileau. He has Maison de Soul Records, over in Ville Platte. Since then my phone rings twenty-four hours a day."

Like Chris Strachwitz, Floyd Soileau is a pivotal figure in the resurgence of zydeco and Cajun music. An animated man who enjoys dancing to the music that he releases, Soileau brings an equal amount of enthusiasm to his dual roles as an astute businessman and a grassroots cultural preservationist. Soileau began recording Cajun music and swamp pop in the 1950s. This was a period of intense assimilation, when the commercial viability of ethnic sounds had hit bottom. Soileau's production of records by Lawrence Walker, D. L. Menard, Nathan Abshire, Belton Richard, and the Balfa Brothers resulted in some of Cajun music's best and most important recordings. His work on Rod Bernard's "This Should Go on Forever," meanwhile, helped make it one of the first swamp pop records to score a national hit, in 1959. But Soileau did not venture into zydeco until the 1970s.

"Around 1975, Clifton Chenier told me that zydeco was the music of the future," Soileau recalled. "I remembered the hard time I had given poor Dewey Balfa about traditional Cajun music, and how I turned him down twice before I recorded him. I said to myself, 'This time, I'm going to listen.' And that's when I started the Maison de Soul label, to concentrate on black Creole music of the area."

The following year, Maison de Soul released *Boogie in Black and White* by Rod Bernard and Clifton Chenier. Soileau acquired and issued some other Chenier material, and began recording such zydeco artists as Rockin' Dopsie, John Delafose, and, in 1984, Boozoo Chavis. In 1985 Soileau released a single entitled "Don't Mess with My Toot-Toot" by the late Rockin' Sidney. A seemingly insignificant zydeco novelty song, "Toot-Toot" became an unexpected hit, and went on a win Grammy Award.

"Rockin' Sidney" Simien had been writing and recording blues, R&B, and swamp pop since the mid-fifties, and enjoyed a career resurgence of sorts in the seventies when "You Ain't Nothin' but Fine" was covered by the popular Texas blues band the Fabulous Thunderbirds. As Simien explained in 1985, his foray into zydeco was purely experimental:

> When I first wrote "Toot-Toot" I had no idea it would go so big. It was one of my first attempts at zydeco, 'cause I'm mainly a rock and roll man. I started out with blues and hillbilly — Muddy Waters, Jimmy Reed, John Lee Hooker, and Little Jimmy Dickens, Hank Williams, Cowboy Copas. Then rock and roll came in, Little Richard and Chuck Berry.

Actually it was considered blues at first, rhythm and blues, and then they started calling it rock and roll.

Eddie Shuler brought it to my attention. "Why don't you try zydeco?" That was around 1980. I have a hang-up because I don't talk French. My people are French, but they talk English. I'm French, but I didn't come up French, my parents didn't teach us French.

Now what made me write "Toot-Toot," I decided to write something that the Cajun people and the Creole people could both relate to. Then I thought about how the word "toot-toot" had been around a long time. I used to hear the guys in the band say *"ma chère toute-toute,"* it seemed they'd always holler that, and *"fais 'tention!,"* they'd use those words, and the audience would seem to get happy when they did. So I put it in a song, and damned if it didn't hit.

I would say it's not typical zydeco, it's a Rockin' Sidney style. I put the accordion in it for a little zydeco/Cajun flavor, and people couldn't say it wasn't French 'cause I had some French words in it. It's a crossover, it could be played on any radio format except classical. It could be pop, soul, country, whatever. I would say its pop-zydeco. It has all the ingredients — it's a gumbo!

When "Don't Mess with My Toot-Toot" was released, there was confusion and controversy as to just what it meant. Some were concerned about drug references, since "toot" was an eighties term for cocaine, although not in this case. Rockin' Sidney's "toot-toot" is an Anglicization of the French word *toute* ("all"), and *"ma chère toute-toute"* translates idiomatically as a term of endearment. The phrase appears in many traditional Creole and Cajun songs, including "Ma Chérie Toute-toute," by the late Cajun fiddler J. B. Fuselier.

Rockin' Sidney remained noncommital on the subject: "A 'toot-toot' is whatever you want it to be" was as much as he would say, but there are definite sexual connotations. Nick Spitzer commented that "a Creole musician explained to me, with some embarrassment, that 'a toot-toot is something underneath a lady's dress.'" Perhaps it was this salacious reading that spurred cover versions by diverse musicians including John Fogerty, R&B singers Denise LaSalle and Jean Knight, and Fats Domino and Doug Kershaw in a duet rendition. The response led Floyd Soileau to arrange a licensing deal with Epic Records, which turned Rockin' Sidney's original version into an unlikely hit on country radio.

Soileau is an astute businessman, and "Don't Mess with My Toot-Toot" made a lot of money both for him and Rockin' Sidney. But Soileau has always remained conscious of his heritage. Reviving the career of Boozoo Chavis was hardly a sure bet, and neither was his 1987 release of John and Alan Lomax's historic field recordings in a two-LP set entitled *Louisiana Cajun and Creole Music—1934: The Lomax Recordings*. Soileau's catalogue also includes an album of Nick Spitzer's folkloric field recordings, entitled *La-La*, released in 1976. These fascinating collections are not big sellers, and their appearance reinforces Soileau's reputation for high integrity in a lowlife industry.

Today Maison de Soul records some of zydeco's most popular new artists, including Keith Frank and Rosie Ledet. Many of these younger bandleaders sing predominately in English, and a debate rages over their musical merits and cultural commitment. But there is no doubt that these stylists help keep young Creole people flocking to the zydeco dance halls.

Boozoo Chavis is unimpressed by such zydeco newcomers—"I been playin' for sixty years," he said dismissively—and he still draws large crowds, including young people, without catering to this new repertoire. Like Clifton Chenier, Chavis takes pride in hard work. A packed dance floor makes Chavis work even harder, and after a few songs he's invariably dripping with sweat. To protect his accordion from perspiration, Boozoo wears a protective apron, which, combined with his ubiquitous Stetson, creates the surrealistic image of Lawrence Welk transformed into a combination cowboy and short-order cook, singing in Creole French. Chavis is a racehorse trainer, and western wear is an important part of his personal aesthetic. "I wear a cowboy hat everywhere I go," he said with pride. "You got to look clean. I don't like them damn hippies, with a scarf on their head, an earbob in their ear, their hair flyin' in their face. Them hippies make me mad. I can't stand them. Me, I wear a cowboy hat everywhere I go. I got that from riding racehorses, training quarterhorses and thoroughbreds."

Many of Chavis's fans also favor cowboy garb. The Creole community's penchant for western regalia gets its fullest expression at the "trail rides," a social function which Chavis actively supports. At these elaborate celebrations several dozen participants ride horses on a long, leisurely course through the countryside, with frequent stops for dancing and visiting at bars, dance halls, and farmhouses. A zydeco band may follow the riders, playing on a flatbed truck; if not, recorded zydeco will resonate, and a live band is likely to play at the final stop, where there will also be a lavish spread of home-cooked food. Trail rides also take place at Mardi Gras, but on a much grander scale. Elaborately costumed riders gallop from farm to farm, collecting ingredients for a communal gumbo and running wild at each stop. Such mayhem has folkloric roots in medieval Europe and the Roman feasts of Lupercalia and Saturnalia. It has also inspired two seasonal anthems—"Le Danse de Mardi Gras" in the Cajun repertoire and a lesser known Creole song, "Chère Camarade."

With his experience and horse sense, Boozoo Chavis is often called to lead and organize trail rides, and he does so with obvious gusto. During the interview at Dog Hill he was preparing for one, and the homestead was abuzz with activity.

Every weekend they got a trail ride somewhere. We sell refreshments to cover some of the expenses. The beer money is supposed to pay for everything, but there's a lot of overhead and you don't know how you're going to come out. You might break even. That boudin sell good, yeah, and the hog cracklin's, and that beer, that beer sell good. And them sandwiches sell good, too.

My wife and I, we been in the trail rides a pretty good while, since about 1982. I had five last year, I organized everything. It's fun, but it's tiresome by the time you come back. I got an Appaloosa horse I ride now, I load him up in that white trailer over there. I go somewhere, people want to shake hands. They say, "Look, Boozoo Chavis is here, we want you to come play for us." I say, "Man, I'm busy, I'm going over yonder," but it makes me feel good. We went to the Big Eight Ride at Grand Prairie, near Jeanerette. I rode the horse twelve miles and my wife followed on the truck. That sun is hot, and the man say, "Let's get a beer, Boozoo." When the horse is walking you can drink it, but then when the ride go fast the beer is foaming up, I don't like wasting it, and you got trouble lighting your cigarette. But when you tie up the horse to that tree, you can relax.

Zydeco trail rides became popular during the 1970s, so they do not preserve an archaic tradition, but their folk roots do run deep.

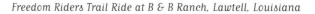

Freedom Riders Trail Ride at B & B Ranch, Lawtell, Louisiana

To the frequent surprise of many visitors, cowboy culture is deeply ingrained in south Louisiana's Creole and Cajun communities. On the rural prairies, horses were a vital energy source for farming and transportation well into the twentieth century. While that need has diminished, the recreational appeal of riding horses remains strong. Riding is also an important practical skill in south Louisiana's extensive cattle-ranching industry, as well as on the racetrack circuit that supported Chavis for decades. As a result, cowboy hats and boots are daily wear for many Creoles and Cajuns alike.

When Creole consciousness emerged during the 1970s, many facets of community life were celebrated, and sometimes they coalesced in new configurations. Creole cowboy culture and zydeco complement each other in an organic blend, and the trail rides have inspired numerous zydeco songs. These include "Boozoo's Trail Ride Breakdown," John T.'s "At the Trail Ride," Chris Ardoin's "Trail Riders," and Morris Francis's "Trail Ride." Most of these songs use a formula based on James Brown's R&B classic "Night Train," which begins

with the announcement "All aboard the night train!" and then calls out the names of cities on a cross-country itinerary. The trail ride ditties follow this pattern by shouting out the names of various south Louisiana towns and/or trail riding clubs.

Trail rides may have also inspired a fad for zydeco songs about mules, as heard on the endless variations of Boozoo Chavis's "Zydeco Hee-Haw." This up-tempo tune vamps on without changing chords, interspersing a catchy ac-

cordion riff with the lone verse: *"Tous les jours sont pas la même chose / Tous les soirs sont pas la même femme"*— "Every day is not the same thing / Every night is not the same woman." The mule noises that follow reflect a swaggering sexuality that recalls such other songs of unbridled passion as "I'm a Jockey," by Chicago blues guitarist Jimmy Johnson, and Mel Tillis's country hit "I Got the Hoss, and You Got the Saddle." After several verse-and-riff se-

Learning the accordion, Lone Plantation Trail Ride at Hamilton's Club

quences, the band "breaks it down" into a churning drum-and-*frottoir* segment, spurred on by snorts, whinnies, and hee-haws. Then the harmonic tension is finally resolved with a shout of *"lâchez-les!"* ("let 'em go!"), and the song gallops off in a dancing frenzy.

Fads aside, the trail rides have a strong connection with early Creole and Cajun music through the lyrical and thematic roots of the words "Hip et Taiau." This line is best known in south Louisiana as the title of a popular Cajun dance song that has been recorded often, under many different French spellings. The title comes from the names of its protagonists: Hip and Taiau, two mischievous dogs who steal various objects—a sled, a hat—from the song's hapless singer, but then return his property to him. (The sled referred to is used for dragging bales of hay.) These nonsensical lyrics represent a seemingly unlikely strain of grassroots surrealism in Cajun music, which can also be heard in such songs as Nathan Abshire's "La valse de Holly Beach":

> The mosquitos ate all of my sweetheart
> They left only her big toes
> For me to use as corks
> To stop up my half-empty wine bottles.
>
> Your papa looks like an elephant
> And your mama like an automobile
> And your small brother resembles a frog
> And your small sister resembles a sidewalk
> corner.

Although the song "Hip et Taiau" is not commonly heard in zydeco, the words "Hip et Taiau" appear frequently, especially in the anthemic "Zydeco sont pas salés." Sometimes the two dogs are merely mentioned by name, as a simple exclamation; sometimes their pranks are recounted, in entirety or in fragments. One of Clifton Chenier's various renditions, transcribed and translated by Ann Allen Savoy, is a case in point:

> Oh, Ma-ma, what did you do with your
> man?
> The snap beans aren't salty

The snap beans aren't salty
They stole my sled,
They stole my sled,
Come a hip and hound
Come a hip and hound

Oh, Ma-ma,
Oh, Ma-ma,
Hey, Ma-ma, oh, Ma-ma
They stole my sled, they stole my sled.

This song intersects with the trail ride/cowboy connection in that the pronunciation of "Hip et Taiau" is strikingly similar to that of the expression "hip-pitiyo," which is found in many folk-rooted cowboy songs and in commercial renditions by Roy Rogers, Gene Autry, Eddie Arnold, and others. There is no firm documentation to prove that this phrase headed west from south Louisiana, but scholars do find the theory plausible.

Many young trail riders are unaware of such traditional roots, and some are naive city slickers with no saddle savvy whatsoever. "A lot of these youngsters, they've probably never been around a horse before," a trail ride organizer told Michael Tisserand. Sometimes such unfamiliarity calls for dramatic cultural immersion, as was the case with L'il Brian Terry, a talented young accordionist from Houston. Attempting to learn more about rural zydeco, Terry went to Eunice, Louisiana, to visit his relatives, the Delafose family. Beyond their extensive musical credentials, he found, his country cousins were also steeped in trail ride culture and horseplay.

"There was a lot of stuff I didn't know about," Terry told Tisserand. "One time Geno Delafose and his cousin Germaine Jack—he's Geno's drummer—decided they were going to teach this city boy a lesson. I was kind of scared of those horses, so they caught me and made me ride. They wrestled me down, threw me on his back, gave the horse a little slap—and he took off."

In the midst of the trail rides' western trappings, a rich African-American folk tradition emerges if Boozoo Chavis is coaxed into singing one of his X-rated hits. These songs come straight from "the dirty dozens," a male bonding genre based on rhyming couplets that boast of macho power and sexual prowess. In one popular recitation known as "Dolomite," the hero describes his "pedigree":

> I got run out of South America for f——in' steers
> I f——ed a she-elephant 'til she broke down in tears
> I swam muddy waters and ain't never got wet
> Mountains has fell on me and I ain't dead yet
> I f——ed an elephant and f——ed her mother
> I can look up a bull's ass and tell you the price of butter
> I f——ed a mother elephant down to a coon
> Even f——ed the same damn cow
> That jumped over the mother f——in' moon."

The dozens can also take the form of competitive sexual insults that are usually directed at the opponent's mother: "I f——ed your mother between two cans / Up jumped a baby and hollered 'Superman!'" Whoever utters the best and final put-down—either a snappy comeback retrieved from memory, or, even better, a spontaneous improvisation—is considered the winner. The ultimate defeat is to be left at a loss for words.

Such material is often strung together in longer recitations known as "toasts." Rudy Ray Moore, a well-known African-American comedian, draws much of his material from this body of folklore, including such classics as "The Signifying Monkey," "The Great Titanic" (also known as "Shine") and his signature recitation, "Dolomite." Characters such as "Peetie Wheatstraw, the Devil's Son-in-Law" appear often in such tales, as does a libidinous character whose exploits are also chronicled by Boozoo Chavis:

> Deacon John, he was a f——in' fool,
> F——ed his teacher on the first day of school
> Lined up a hundred women 'gainst the wall
> Bet a hundred dollars he could f—— 'em all
> Then he died and he went to hell,
> He f——ed the devil and his wife as well
> He looked at me and he looked at you,
> Bet you five dollars gonna f—— you, too!

As the band repeats the vocal phrase "Deacon John," Chavis echoes it with a rhythmic figure on his accordion, merging zydeco with the dirty dozens. When this material is performed as an a capella spoken presentation, it is generally recited as a single unit, but Chavis separates it into couplets that are divided by short instrumental intervals.

The flip side of "Deacon John" is the equally risqué "Uncle Bud":

> Eighteen, nineteen, twenty years ago,
> Uncle Bud beat the shit out of Cotton-Eyed Joe

> Uncle Bud got this, Uncle Bud got that,
> Uncle Bud got a pecker like a baseball bat!

This format and many of these interchangeable couplets have been used by blues artists and comedians since the dawn of recording. In the 1930s the great slide guitarist Kokomo Arnold recorded a particularly graphic version of "The Dirty Dozens," while pianist Roosevelt Sykes never failed to please crowds with his raunchy and thinly veiled "Dirty Mother for You." The late actor Redd Foxx launched his career as a stand-up comedian by performing such material,

and he later brought a similarly sly sensibility, minus the four-letter words and overt sexuality, to the television series *Sanford and Son.* During the seventies and eighties, Richard Pryor's caustic humor also drew on this tradition. Themes and lyrics that date back decades in this genre are continually recycled, as heard on such comparatively recent blues hits as Clarence Carter's "Strokin'" and "Love Her with a Feelin'." They also live on in the work of contemporary black comedians including Chris Rock and Don "D. C." Curry.

Boozoo Chavis is picky about where and when he performs such material, and sometimes he opts for milder renditions, such as "Unce Bud beat the heck out of Cotton-Eyed Joe," or "Uncle Bud got *something* [italics added] like a baseball bat!"

At some places they like for me to play the song, but they want me to play it "good." They say, "We got a bunch of them old ladies in here so keep it clean. But then them old ladies ask me to play it "bad." And I say, "I can't, I can't play it bad, I won't!" But that's what they want. If I go to Slim's Y-Ki-Ki, in Opelousas, I hold back, I play it good, then on the last part I might drop the bad words in there, and they start whooping it up. They say, "Play it like you made the record!" Oh, they get mad if you don't want to play it bad. One night I played it good, then I cut loose on that son-of-a-gun and I played it bad. My wife turned around and she looked at me. She acted like she had got mad. She don't care, her, but she got ashamed for me, she didn't want me to play that for them people.

Boozoo Chavis does not like to offend his audiences' sense of propriety, but he is never ashamed of his own blunt opinions. This trait certainly emerged during our long chat at Dog Hill.

I know music. I can't read music, but I know it by ear, I listen to it. Now I like zydeco, but I like them blues, too, B. B. King and all of them. Sam Cooke, before he got killed, I like him, I got his tape in my truck.

And then I like country music, I like Hank Williams, Hank Williams *Senior.* But his boy can't play like him. He got a good record contract and all that, but he'll never play like his daddy. He had one or two songs that sound like his daddy, but then he go playing that old hippie stuff, and that ain't no good. But his daddy used to play "Your cheatin' heart will tell on you," his daddy could sing and play the guitar. Shit. I know music, yeah.

Now in zydeco I like Clifton Chenier's music and I tell you, the people don't like John Delafose, but I like John Delafose's music. And I like Buckwheat's music. And I like Willis

Boozoo Chavis on horseback

Prudhomme. You know, he's kind of a bright fellow [light-skinned], wear a cowboy hat, he is just as nice as he can be. Fernest and the Thunders used to be good, but I never hear him no more. Preston Frank, he's pretty good, yeah. Terrance Simien, I like his music, yeah, but sometimes he play too wild.

You ask me if I'm surprised to see zydeco come back, today, 1987? No, sir. It don't surprise me, no. What brought it back? I guess it's the future, I don't know how to explain it. But it sure come back. I guess the people got a little wiser, a little smarter. And they got youngsters at my dances and old people, too, all together, all dancing to my music — Friday, Saturday, Sunday — and they love it. It make me feel good. They want to follow that French music, that zydeco. And they speaking that French language, that's coming back, too.

As the zydeco resurgence hurtles on, Boozoo Chavis resolutely sticks to his archaic rural style. He remains oblivious to passing trends, except those that he has started himself. Chavis has been immortalized in song, on such numbers as NRBQ's "Boozoo, That's Who" and "I Got It from Boo," by zydeco neophyte JoJo Reed. Chavis's stature is also underscored by his mock rivalry with a rising zydeco star named Beau Jocque. This faux feud has been played out on the southwest Louisiana dance hall circuit, at the Zydeco Festival in Plaisance, and most notably at New Orleans's leading zydeco venue, the Mid-City Bowling Lanes—also known as the Rock 'n' Bowl—where the two had a bowling contest that Chavis won. "We're fakes," Beau Jocque told Michael Tisserand, "like professional wrestlers. It was all in fun." Even so, Chavis put a typically feisty spin on the relationship.

"Beau Jocque just come out on the circuit," Chavis told radio announcer Haydée Lafaye Ellis. "Beau Jocque got a name right now. And some folks now, they want to put Beau Jocque *over* me. I don't like that, and I'll tell the world that. I'm not jealous of Beau Jocque, no. Last night someone told me, said, 'Boozoo, Beau Jocque can't stand next to you.' Well, I know that already. Shit. I been playing music for sixty years!"

Occasionally such healthy self-esteem goes well over the top. As Chavis told Peter Watrous of the *New York Times,* "Sometimes I'm on stage looking at all those people dancing, and I feel sorry for them. I say to myself, 'After you die, Boozoo, there ain't gonna be no more like you.' This is the best they've ever heard. I'm a genius, no doubt about it."

If Boozoo Chavis didn't emanate genuine warmth along with such irascible bluster, he would simply sound arrogant. But Chavis has paid his dues, more than most. Before reemerging, he was known only to devotees of obscure records. His debut recordings, which had been reissued on an esoteric blues anthology in 1968, soon went out of print again. As a collector of such albums, I was amazed to learn in 1984 that Boozoo Chavis was still alive, let alone that he had actively resumed performing. His comeback has immeasurably enriched zydeco, and opened vast opportunities for ensuing generations. As Chavis gazes at the world from Dog Hill, he can justly revel in his considerable accomplishments:

I come a long way from picking cotton and hoein'. I used to couldn't afford a book of matches. One can of pork and beans had to make it for the whole family. All the nice things I got now, music paid for them. You see, I always knew I could do it, but I never got no recognition. I wanted to show the world what I could do. I always knew that once people heard me, they'd know different. Now that we're traveling, we're opening people's eyes. They're sayin', "Where he come from, that little man? That joker can *play.*"

Geno Delafose at Slim's Y–Ki–Ki

Cowboys watch dancers at Richard's Club

Miss Ann Goodly at Gilton's Club, Eunice, Louisiana

"Papa Paul" Goodly and his dog, Jack, at Papa Paul's Club, Mamou, Louisiana

"Slim" Gradney, owner of Slim's Y–Ki–Ki, c. 1989

Sandra Serile, bassist with Delton Broussard and the Lawtell Playboys, at Papa Paul's Club

Left: Herbert and Jeffery Broussard of Zydeco Force at the B & B Ranch, Lawtell, Louisiana
Above: Paul "A'Pillion" Harris

Above: Lawrence and Chris Ardoin, c. 1987
Right: Side door at Richard's Club

Delton Broussard

Preston Frank and his family band at a church dance in Basile, Louisiana

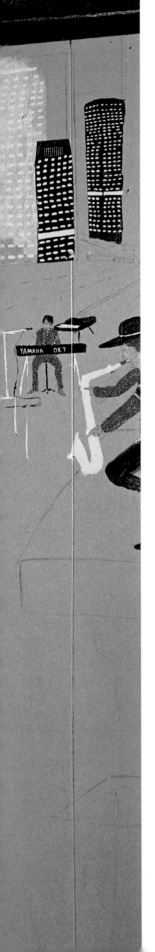

Left: Ambrose Sam and Leon Sam at Truman's Place, Lafayette, Louisiana

Above: Hiram Sampy, leader of Sampy and the Bad Habits

Woman leaning on car at Slim's Y–Ki–Ki

Fernest Arceneaux at Richard's Club

Left: Dieudonne "Double D" Dauphine at the Dauphine Club, Parks, Louisiana
Above: Cooking gumbo at the Dauphine Club

Celebrating
Creole
Identity

**Buckwheat Zydeco:
Mainstream Ambassador**

Along with Clifton Chenier and Boozoo Chavis, there is a third hero among contemporary zydeco musicians: Stanley "Buckwheat" Dural. Born in Lafayette in 1947, Dural uses the stage name Buckwheat Zydeco; he acquired the moniker "Buckwheat" as a child, from the character in the television program *The Little Rascals*. Dural is revered for his ability, his active encouragement of younger players, and his deserved, enviable success. No other zydeco musician works on a comparable career level. One especially striking example was Dural's nationally televised performance during the closing ceremonies for the 1996 summer Olympics in Atlanta. In the summer of 1998 Dural and his band performed with the Boston Pops Orchestra; the concert was broadcast live on the A & E cable television network. Dural has also made the rounds of all the national television talk shows, and has toured as the opening act for rock stars such as U2 and Eric Clapton.

Dural has also recorded with Eric Clapton, as well as with Willie Nelson, Dwight Yoakam, Keith Richards, Los Lobos, and gospel singer Mavis Staples. A four-time Grammy nominee, he was the first zydeco artist to sign with a major record label. Dural has provided music for numerous film soundtracks and commercials for products including Coca-Cola, Cheerios, and Budweiser. His performance fee is considerably higher than that of his zydeco colleagues, who still travel the highways in crowded vans while Dural cruises in the comfort of a bus. But while Dural moves in celebrity circles and maintains a sophisticated Web site — www.buckwheatzydeco.com — he has always kept close ties with the Creole community. His prominence, in fact, allows him to serve as one of its most vocal cultural activists.

Although Dural is a consummate musician, there are other zydeco artists who approach his level of talent. But success in the music industry takes far more than mere ability; professional representation is equally important. Dural was fortunate enough to make a connection with Ted Fox, a New York music writer who became fascinated with zydeco while researching an article for *Audio* magazine. Fox appreciated zydeco's potential for broad appeal, and noticed that no one was attempting to develop it. He decided to step into the breach. Switching careers, in a zydeco version of Jon Landau meets Bruce

Springsteen, Fox left journalism in 1986 to become Dural's manager.

Dural, for his part, had the good sense to see that working with Fox was a smart move and a big break, instead of yet another music industry scam. He was not burdened by the old school mentality, personified by his former boss, Clifton Chenier, in which suspicion resulting from bitter experience leads artists to trust no one but themselves. Time constraints alone make self-management impractical; performing, recording, traveling, and being interviewed are exhausting enough for musicians, without their having to organize all of the innumerable details involved, as well as pushing for higher career levels. In addition, few self-managed artists can effectively cultivate business contacts or command respect in negotiations.

Nevertheless, a stubborn do-it-yourself mentality persists among many other zydeco musicians, as it does in many traditional stylistic camps. After his appearance on Paul Simon's *Graceland,* for instance, Rockin' Dopsie turned down an invitation to play on *Saturday Night Live.* He simply had never heard of the popular television program, and told the booker, "That night I got a church dance in Houston." Dural and Fox enjoy a good rapport, however, and do not squander such golden opportunities. When they teamed up, Dural had already recorded several albums for Louisiana companies such as Jay Miller's Blues Unlimited, and the then-fledgling Black Top label in New Orleans. Dural had followed Clifton Chenier's example of bringing diverse songs into zydeco. While Chenier had little interest in material created after the 1960s, however, Dural's approach was more current and eclectic. More significantly, Dural had just released his second album for Rounder Records. This company, based in Cambridge, Massachusetts, was among the first out-of-state labels to aggressively mine the 1980s resurgence of zydeco, Cajun music, New Orleans R&B, and the modernized brass band jazz of such groups as the Dirty Dozen. Most of these albums were produced by Scott Billington, whose ongoing work is a major influence on all of these styles. Many of today's most popular zydeco artists — Nathan Williams, Geno Delafose, Beau Jocque, L'il Brian Terry — might not have emerged without Billington's vision.

In 1985 Billington produced Dural's Rounder album, *Waitin' for My Ya-Ya.*

Its title track was a reggae adaptation of an R&B hit by New Orleans singer Lee Dorsey, and the timing couldn't have been better. Ted Fox was finishing work on a book entitled *In the Groove*. Published the following year, *In the Groove* was an anthology of interviews with noted record producers and entrepreneurs. One of Fox's subjects was Chris Blackwell of Island Records, whose many accomplishments included the popularization of reggae in America through his work with such seminal artists as Bob Marley and Jimmy Cliff. The parallels between reggae and zydeco were striking. Both were ethnic dance music, rooted in infectious Caribbean rhythms, with lyrics that few mainstream American listeners could decipher. These esoteric qualities increased reggae's exotic appeal, and were emphasized to enhance its marketing. Fox pointed out the connections to Blackwell, and made the case that the similarities could well extend to sales. Blackwell responded by offering Dural a five-album deal with Island and suggesting that he hire Ted Fox to serve as his manager and producer.

Dural's first Island album, *On a Night Like This,* was recorded in suburban New Orleans in the spring of 1987. Throughout several days of recording, Fox directed the proceedings with a single drumstick that he held like a conductor's baton. Dural was suffering from swollen feet, and soaked them in a plastic bucket between takes. These unusual sights belied the duo's carefully crafted plan. Although Fox had no formal production experience, he knew his music, and had a clear vision of what would put Dural across: a combination of Creole roots and material that was already familiar to rock audiences. This concept also fuels Fox's insistence that Buckwheat Zydeco's albums be stocked in the rock section at record stores, where they have a far better chance of being purchased.

On a Night Like This opened with a scorching version of "Ma 'Tit Fille." Sung in French, with lots of spoken asides, it had a swaggering shuffle tempo and boisterous horn arrangements that were written by Dural and performed by the Dirty Dozen Brass Band. "Ma 'Tit Fille" was based on a number known both as "Ma Négresse" and "Pine Grove Blues," that had been popularized by Cajun accordionist Nathan Abshire, as well as by Clifton Chenier. Buckwheat's inter-

pretation was grounded in these renditions, yet strictly contemporary. Fox balanced this zydeco vérité by choosing a Bob Dylan song as the title track and by "zydeco-izing" an up-tempo tune entitled "Marie, Marie" by the Blasters, a now-defunct rock band that was very popular at the time.

During the sixties this calculated catering to youthful rock audiences often failed miserably. Unsympathetic producers forced traditional artists to record contemporary material that they disliked and performed poorly, under obvious duress. Some truly embarrassing blues albums collapsed under the weight of such contrivance. In 1968, the harmonica player and singer Howlin' Wolf was forced to record a pseudo-psychedelic set for Chess Records entitled *Electric Wolf*. He complained to *Rolling Stone* that it sounded like "dog shit." But with *On a Night Like This*, this cultural blend worked seamlessly, thanks to Dural's versatility and the wise choice of songs.

"This album is different than anything I ever did before," Dural said, immersed

up to his ankles in Epsom salts. "This one has more of a mixture, mixing in some pop and R&B, more of a 'now generation' thing, but there's traditional zydeco, too. Those new tunes, like the Dylan song, they clicked, but they were hard to adapt to at first." Dural paused to reflect for a moment, and then hit on one of the most crucial factors in the album's artistic success. "This is the first time that I ever did rehearsal for an album," he said. (The band and Fox had spent a week "woodshedding" at a zydeco club called Paul's Playhouse in the small town of Sunset, outside Lafayette.) "Usually we just go in the studio and let things happen. That's how it's been on every other album I recorded. You can hear the difference. They took time with the setup and the recording, too. The sound quality is a lot better, and I like that."

On a Night Like This also featured a zydeco treatment of the classic Memphis soul instrumental "Time Is Tight," originally recorded by Booker T. and the M.G.s. This was a significant choice because, like Booker T. Jones, Dural had started his career as a soul music keyboardist. Although Dural had grown up in a household full of zydeco, at the time he hated it with a passion.

"My dad played the accordion every day," Dural told Michael Tisserand. "You better believe every day, that's how come I was sick of the accordion. Morning, before he'd leave to go to work. Come to lunch, the accordion. At night, accordion. Next night, accordion." Buckwheat's father, Stanley Dural, Sr., never played zydeco in public, preferring to entertain at family gatherings. But he wanted his namesake son to do so, once it became evident that Stanley, Jr., had been born with musical talent. Buckwheat would have none of it. "I was truly against this stuff," he told journalist Todd Mouton. "I was against zydeco, period—I'm serious."

Dural learned to play piano from an older brother, and by the age of nine he was working at local nightclubs. The versatile Lynn August, who later took up the accordion, backed Dural on drums. By junior high school Dural had joined a band called Sammy and the Untouchables, opening shows for such prominent R&B artists as Fats Domino and Ray Charles, whose hits are still important components in Buckwheat Zydeco's repertoire. After graduating from high school, Dural worked the Gulf Coast soul and R&B circuit in the bands of singer Joe Tex, singer and guitarist Barbara Lynn, and multi-instrumentalist Clarence "Gate-mouth" Brown.

Feeling stifled as an accompanist, Dural formed his own band, Buckwheat and the Hitchhikers, in 1971. Fronting a fifteen-piece band and a five-voice chorus, Dural played Hammond B-3 organ, cranking out up-to-the-minute funk hits by the likes of Parliament/Funkadelic, Earth Wind & Fire, the Ohio Players, and James Brown. "James was an inspiration," Dural explained to Michael Tisserand. "He was telling us, 'This is who you are, don't be ashamed of it.' When he made the song 'Say It Loud, I'm Black and I'm Proud,' that meant a lot to me."

Dural has taken a similar yet more specific stance on the issue of Creole identity and the importance of distinguishing it from Cajun culture. The issue crystallized for him during a two-and-a-half-year tenure as Clifton Chenier's organist. When Buckwheat and the Hitchhikers disbanded, Chenier offered Dural a job that returned him full circle to his father's beloved zydeco. "Me and my dad had a big problem," Dural told Tisserand. "He'd never been out to see me perform. He'd say, 'It's no-good music, what you're playing. You need to play music like Clifton Chenier.' And I was one of the biggest critics of accordion music, but I wouldn't tell that to him. In my generation, you don't tell that to your dad."

Dural absorbed lots of zydeco technique from Chenier and some deeper personal lessons as well. "What I learned from him was that this is your culture, this is your roots, and don't be ashamed of it," he told Tisserand. Chenier, for his part, was fond of dispensing fatherly advice. He closed our 1983 interview with this message to his public: "Be what you are, do what you think is best, and always have confidence in your own self. And if you gonna do something, do it *right*."

Inspired by Chenier and perceiving zydeco's growing momentum, Dural left Chenier's band in 1978 and spent eight months practicing in seclusion. He adapted his horizontal keyboard skills to the vertical realm of the chromatic accordion, and worked on singing lead without the assistance of a five-voice chorus. When Dural felt ready, he struck out on his own as Buckwheat Zydeco, in 1979. This stage name alone made a statement about his Creole identity, but Dural reinforced it by calling his group the Ils Sont Partis Band. *"Ils sont partis!"*—"they're off!"—is the announcement made at local racetracks when the horses leave the starting gate. It is an appropriate metaphor for Dural's exhilarating

music, and the use of French implies that listeners must attempt to understand the music on Dural's own Creole terms.

Dural felt confident and primed for success when he met Ted Fox a few years later. Their partnership began to gather momentum just as America's fascination with south Louisiana was also accelerating. This process, in turn, came on the heels of south Louisiana's internal cultural renaissance. In the mid-1980s a burgeoning interest in the region intensified rapidly because of two factors: the ascendance of Chef Paul Prudhomme's nouvelle Cajun cuisine and the popularity of the film *The Big Easy.* The net effect of both was positive, especially in terms of the economic opportunities offered to Cajuns and Creoles alike. But neither fad presented an accurate depiction of daily life in Creole and Cajun country.

Prudhomme's creations were innovative, delicious, and deservedly well received. But they were personal inventions that used regional cuisine as a mere point of departure. Cajun and Creole home cooking includes such toothsome staples as gumbo, courtbouillon, étouffée, cochon du lait, and fricassée, but not "blackened" redfish, which was Prudhomme's signature dish. During the Cajun food craze that followed Prudhomme's success, restaurants across the country served up bizarre, blackened entrées that were charred and peppered beyond recognition. In Louisiana, such food is sold mainly to tourists.

There was a similar sense of Cajun overkill in the wake of *The Big Easy.* To its credit, the 1987 film catapulted south Louisiana music into the national lime-

Wilbert Guillory at the Southwest Louisiana Zydeco Festival, Plaisance, Louisiana

light, with a sound track album that included Buckwheat Zydeco's "Ma 'Tit Fille," along with songs by BeauSoleil and a then-unknown zydeco band called Terrance Simien and the Mallet Playboys. All three bands benefitted directly, local music blossomed, and venues around the globe started booking Cajun, zydeco, and New Orleans artists. The Louisiana music community is indebted to composer and saxophonist Dickie Landry, who convinced director Jim McBride to set the film in south Louisiana and fill it with regional sounds.

At its core, however, *The Big Easy* was a rather trite murder mystery. Dennis Quaid played the lead role with charisma and intensity, but the local accent that he affected was ridiculous. Attempting to combine Cajun cadences with the unique strains of New Orleans, he came up with a strange hybrid that failed on both counts. This was an innocent enough mistake, in the light entertainment context of a popular summer movie — but, like blackened redfish, it was accepted as authentic outside of Louisiana. As the popularity of *The Big Easy* soared at the box office, the movie's other implied misconceptions took hold. South Louisiana and Cajun country were presented as synonymous, with New Orleans portrayed as their principal city. Anything or anyone with a Cajun name or connection was instantly perceived as chic, exotic, and desirable. Cajuns and non-Cajuns alike exploited this mania by "Cajun-izing" every product in sight, frantically cashing in before the fad faded. One result was resentment among many Creoles, who felt that the Cajun half of south Louisiana's populace was receiving all of the profits and publicity.

With Dural's approval, Ted Fox issued this press release in 1988:

> To our promoters, producers, club owners, etc.: I manage and produce Buckwheat Zydeco, and I'd like to thank you for your support and interest. Amazing things are happening to this band as more and more people are boogieing to the Buckwheat beat. And as our popularity grows, it becomes more important that certain basic information about the band and zydeco in general be understood and disseminated correctly.
>
> First, please do not use the word Cajun in connection with Buck or zydeco music. Cajuns are the *white* descendants of the original French settlers of Nova Scotia, which was originally known as Acadia (that's where the word Cajun comes from). Buckwheat, and all the French-speaking black people of southwestern Louisiana, refer to themselves as *Creole*. Zydeco music is not Cajun music, although there are some similarities. Please

refer to zydeco as "Creole dance music" or "Louisiana's hottest music" or whatever you like, but not Cajun music.

This is a serious cultural issue with Buck. That's why our performance contracts contain the following warning hand-stamped in large red type: DO NOT use the word "CAJUN" to promote/advertise this show. Such use is STRICTLY PROHIBITED and will void this contract.

Calling Buck a Cajun is sort of like calling an Irishman English, and referring to zydeco as Cajun music is like calling reggae calypso music.

Second, the band is not from New Orleans, and zydeco is not New Orleans music. The band, as well as most zydeco bands, is based in and around the small city of Lafayette, which is over a hundred miles west of New Orleans — on the other side of the Mississippi River and the great Atchafalaya Swamp. Once again, it is as distinct a difference as Jamaica is from Trinidad, or Ireland is from England.

We greatly appreciate your keeping this in mind in your advertisements, promotions, and publicity, and we look forward to making the next Buckwheat Zydeco show as hot as you can handle.

Fox's intent was accuracy and respect, not divisiveness. His statement parallels some remarks made by the late Cajun fiddler Dewey Balfa: "My culture is not better than anybody else's culture. My people were no better than anybody else. And yet I will not accept it as a second-class culture. It's my culture. It's the best culture for me. Now, I would expect that if you have a different culture, that you would feel the same about yours as I feel about mine." Balfa was one of the first and most eloquent advocates of Cajun culture, and this sensibility included an appreciative respect for "la musique créole" and zydeco. He recorded with Bois-sec Ardoin and Canray Fontenot, appeared on an album with Rockin' Dopsie, and often played the festival circuit with zydeco artists.

William Hamilton of Hamilton's Club mixing hog slop

Stanley "Buckwheat" Dural is the most visible crusader for zydeco/Creole identity, but there are others who are equally vocal. One of the most active and effective is Wilbert Guillory, the director emeritus and cofounder of the Southwest Louisiana Zydeco Festival. Emerging in the early eighties and currently directed by Liz Savoy Guillory, this grassroots gathering has become a regional highlight of the Labor Day weekend. It is presented by the Southern Development Foundation, an agricultural cooperative with branch offices in several southern states. The foundation focuses primarily on the economic health of African-American farmers, and maintains several large properties for conducting crop research. One such farm near Plaisance, Louisiana, also serves as the festival's site.

Wilbert Guillory, a veteran of the civil rights movement of the 1960s, is a committed champion of Creole culture. Like Dural and many other black Americans, he was profoundly affected by James Brown's message of black pride. As Guillory explained, Brown's statement resonates with his own personal mission:

> What I want to spend the rest of my life doing is encourage people who still can speak Creole to continue to dig into our inheritance. We have a lot of culture out there that we need to know about as black Creoles, and a lot more to learn about our identity. Since I've learned more about myself I'm a much happier person. I'm proud of who I am.
>
> My role is to let people know very strongly that I'm not a Cajun, to let them know, no matter what anyone says, that zydeco is not Cajun music. It is black Afro-American Creole music. Because I am a Creole. That's my best language, Creole French, which is different from Cajun French. So there's no way that I can accept myself as a Cajun, I'm not. I'm Creole and I was born in a small Creole community called Pointe Noire.
>
> It's funny, I always did accept myself as black, but when I was coming up, you didn't call no black person "black," that was an insult. We would use "colored," "colored people," *"les gens de couleur."* White people were *"les blancs,"* we wasn't 'sposed to call no white person "Cajun," either, that was an insult, you was gonna have a fight.
>
> Now when black people really started being proud of themselves is when James Brown started singing "I'm Black and I'm Proud." It made a very big impression, all over the country, and that's when I realized, "Hey, this guy is right, we *are* black and we *are* proud."

The community that Guillory celebrates consists mainly of people from rural areas or small towns. They speak French, ride horses, and wear cowboy hats.

A door prize of feed and tack awaits a winner as Roy Carrier plays at Richard's Club

This contrasts sharply with the one-dimensional depictions of black Americans as inner-city residents, a stereotype that also encompasses poverty, ignorance, and violent crime. Guillory continued:

My background is in farming. I been in farming all my life. I started out as a sharecropper. I raised sweet potatoes, and us small farmers couldn't compete with the big farms, so we organized a cooperative of sweet potato farmers to get better prices. Eventually we hooked up with Louisiana State University, and started doing agricultural and horticultural experiments on a plot of land that I own. We got some grants from the Ford Foundation and some federal money when President Carter was in office. But then when Reagan came in, that all got wiped out. But we proved that a small farmer could make a living if he was given a fair chance.

The Southern Development Foundation is connected with the Southern Cooperative Development Fund. They help small farmers get loans, and then the Southern Development Foundation provides technical assistance. The Fund works in a bunch of different states in the South. Louisiana is the only state where they're pushing zydeco, 'cause this is where zydeco comes from. But they work with another music festival that's run by the local black community. That's the Delta Blues Festival, in Greenville, Mississippi. It's getting pretty big, pretty popular. It's run by an organization called M.A.C.E., the Mississippi Association for Community Enrichment. They're members of the Southern Development Foundation, too. One of their people, Vanessa Green, helped us start our festival.

It's both significant and appropriate that zydeco's leading community-based event is produced by an organization devoted to family farming. If the link between the two seems unlikely at first, a closer look reveals logical connections, much like those between zydeco, cowboy culture, and the trail rides. Zydeco's name derives from a vegetable, a product of the soil. A band from Lafayette called the Creole Zydeco Farmers gets plenty of work, and Clifton Chenier used to proudly sing a number entitled "Je suis un recoulteur" — "I'm a Farmer." On a deeper level, many Creoles and Cajuns are rural residents, and even those who do not farm for a living often plant extensive vegetable gardens, butcher their own meat, and go fishing in order to fill the family freezer, rather than for mere recreation. Such self-reliance was crucial when the region was isolated and money was scarce, and it remains ingrained in the fierce

local work ethic. As Barry Ancelet observed, both Cajun music and zydeco have "dirt beneath their nails."

"I used to go hunting rabbits with a stick," Stanley "Buckwheat" Dural told Michael Tisserand. "And that was a meal for me, my brothers and sisters, my mom and dad. You hear what I'm telling you? I used to hunt armadillos, possum, and nutria. I'm a woodsman. If nature is there, I will survive."

Self-reliance is crucial to the agenda of another organization that nurtures the Zydeco Festival—a cultural awareness association known as C.R.E.O.L.E., Inc., which was founded during the 1980s. Its acronym stands for the somewhat cumbersome Cultural Resource Education of Linguistic Enrichment. If the name is rather awkward, the mission statement is sound: the group intends "to develop the Creole language and culture in Louisiana. This culture has been a major contributor to the foods, music, language, and spirit of south Louisiana. Its richness merits acknowledgement and preservation."

One of C.R.E.O.L.E., Inc.'s cofounders was John Broussard. Broussard recently retired from the Farmers Home Administration, where he performed duties that were similar to those handled by the Southern Development Founda-

Paul Scott backstage at the Southwest Louisiana Zydeco Festival

tion. He remains actively involved both with C.R.E.O.L.E., Inc., and the Zydeco Festival, and hosts a Saturday morning zydeco show on KVRS-FM in Lafayette.

We want to promote cultural exchange with groups of other black, French-speaking people. We want to connect with the other Creoles from Africa and the Caribbean. We host visiting journalists from those countries, and introduce them to our food and our Creole zydeco music. We would like to assist in the development of tourism in south Louisiana, bring in tourists from the Creole countries and from around the world.

I want to emphasize that C.R.E.O.L.E., Inc., is not anti-Cajun. The Cajuns have plenty to be proud of, no question about it. If we were anti-Cajun, we would be denying some of our own identity, since we all speak French. We simply want to promote our culture along with that of the Cajuns. And the response to us from Cajuns is very positive, along the lines of "You should have done this long ago, to promote your particular corner of this bigger French culture." We also feel that the news media needs to recognize all segments of the community and realize that as black people we are not Cajuns, even though we do have a lot in common.

Some zydeco enthusiasts are surprised to learn that the Zydeco Festival is also supported by the Catholic Church. One of the festival's founders is a priest, Father A. J. McKnight, who remains actively involved in the event itself and in the work of the Southern Development Foundation. This support also functions in a broader sense. The Creoles and Cajuns of southwestern Louisiana are predominately Catholic, and the church has a long history of nurturing zydeco. Church halls are often used for zydeco dances, as evidenced by Clifton Chenier's album *Live at St. Mark's*. Houston's Creole community hosts a regular circuit of Catholic church hall dances that are scheduled cooperatively to avoid competition.

Despite this connection, Wilbert Guillory experienced some emotional conflicts between his devout Catholicism and his Creole advocacy:

When I was young I used to walk about eight miles just to get to church on Sunday. We would walk barefoot until we got close to the

---

Stanley "Buckwheat" Dural at Tee's Connection, St. Martinville, Louisiana

church, wipe our feet with a towel, put our shoes back on and then walk in. I would say my prayers in Creole, until I grew up to be a little older, 'cause I didn't know how to speak English at all until I started school. Then they retaught me my prayers in English so I could make my first communion. In church I would see all of these images — the Crucifix, the Mother of God, the stations of the cross — and everyone was lily white. As I got older that turned me off, and I stopped going to church for about ten years.

The Zydeco Festival's growth gives Guillory a sense of accomplishment that extends beyond the festival to incorporate the philosophy of the civil rights struggle. "The goal that we really set up," he explained, "was to recognize the black Creole artists, and I think we've done that. And this is a nice, family festival, like a big family reunion. It was organized by local people, and it's controlled by local people. We have corporate sponsors, but they don't come in and change our idea of what we want to do."

These sentiments are shared by Paul Scott, who books the bands for the events and performs a similar function for the Festival International de Louisiane. This annual mid-April event in Lafayette, founded in 1987, combines a core of south Louisiana music with multimedia performers from every corner of the French-speaking world. Like the Zydeco Festival, Festival International has enriched community pride and reinforced the concept of a global French community. As Scott explained:

Both festivals help each other. We've brought international attention to the country people of southwestern Louisiana, and that's what this is really all about, down-home country people. And that includes the Cajun people too, now, you got to accept the way history laid it down, because those accordions didn't come here from the Ivory Coast. The Creoles and the Cajuns borrowed from each other, and we each put our own influence on the French language and the music. It's a give-and-take thing.

What's interesting to me is how zydeco music has come full circle in some ways. Ten years ago the young musicians all used to play piano accordions and pattern themselves on Clifton and Buckwheat. Of course, that was great. But now a lot of the new bandleaders are playing single-row accordions like Amédé Ardoin did back in the old days. I'm not saying all the young guys are as good as Amédé, not everybody supports what they're doing, some of those popular dudes like Keith Frank. But a young person can make a good living playing zydeco today. It didn't used to be that way, definitely not. I think our festival has helped everything grow and still stay genuine to our Creole roots.

Genuine Creole roots are equally important to Stanley "Buckwheat" Dural. A hectic schedule notwithstanding, he is generous with his time when it comes to teaching younger players or helping the local community. "Buckwheat's a terrific guy," testified his protégé, Nathan Williams. "You're not going to find many musicians who will try to help you. Most of them are gonna be jealous, and keep all the attention for themselves."

No matter what career heights Dural may reach, he does so on his own cultural terms. "I didn't come this far," he told Michael Tisserand, "by saying that I'm someone I'm not. If you don't have that identity, man, you're just lost. How could someone say that this area is Cajun country? You have black, you have white, you have some Indians, Vietnamese, and we're all here in Louisiana, we all make Louisiana work. And please believe me, I know. I pay more taxes than the average person in Louisiana. I'm not passing through here, I live here — and I won't accept it."

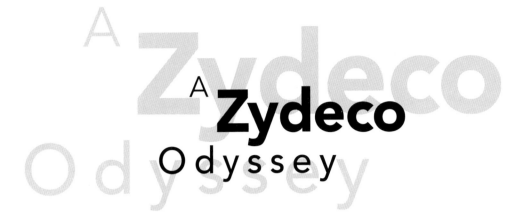

A Zydeco Odyssey

Warren Ceasar's
Long Journey Home

Although Stanley "Buckwheat" Dural stands apart in terms of success, many aspects of his career are shared by other zydeco musicians who were also born during the 1940s and 1950s. Immersed from birth in Creole music and culture, they went through a natural phase of separation by pursuing other styles, especially soul music and rhythm and blues. There was also a pragmatic reason for such experimentation, because zydeco fell on tough times during the sixties, offering few career opportunities. Zydeco ultimately came back stronger than ever, and musicians returned to the fold with both sentimental and mercenary motives. Clifton Chenier's son C. J. followed this circuitous path, as did fellow accordionists Lynn August and Fernest Arceneaux. But one of the most striking such sagas in zydeco is that of trumpeter Warren Ceasar, a former member of Clifton Chenier's Red Hot Louisiana Band and one of the few zydeco bandleaders who does not play the accordion. In a series of interviews over home-cooked gumbo and catfish courtbouillon, Ceasar described his long journey home.

Zydeco is where I grew up, hey, I was seven years old when I went to the la-las, every Saturday night, with Bois-sec and Canray Fontenot, Canray is my uncle. I grew up in Basile, I'm from Basile, around Big Mamou back there, a little community called L'Anse Maigre. I grew up there on a plantation, my daddy was a sharecropper. I was born in 1952.

These la-las I went to was at a nightclub. Bois-sec Ardoin had a nightclub, the Cowboy Club, in Duralde, that's a little community between Basile and Eunice. Back in those days I was picking cotton for Bois-sec, too, man. Oh, yeah, I picked cotton, I dug sweet potatoes, I didn't cut no cane, but I did farm with my dad, he planted rice, soybeans. And my dad had a piece of land to plant his own corn and his beans, potatoes, okra.

Bois-sec and my uncle Canray Fontenot, they always did have a band. And the same time, well, Bois-sec was getting his sons into the band. I was a little guy, I was seven years old, running around the clubs and stuff and I didn't know anything about no la-la. I was twenty-five or twenty-six years old, when I discovered that hey, this la-la, this is zydeco music.

I was just born with music, as a gift from God. The first instrument I started playing was saxophone. I wanted to be a saxophone player, but my old man didn't want to give me fifty cents a day for the reeds, you know, the reed was a very delicate little piece of wood, and you break it, you in trouble. When you a kid, you don't realize the value of fifty cents. So what happened, my brother had graduated from high school, and he played the cornet, this old beat-up cornet my daddy had bought him for twenty-five or thirty bucks. So he stashed his cornet in the closet, dig, and he hauled ass off to St. Louis.

I was halfway playing drums 'cause I couldn't afford to buy the reeds for the saxophone. One day I just got frustrated with getting a bunch of cardboard boxes together and beating on them with pieces of wood. But I couldn't afford to buy the reeds for the saxophone. I went in the closet, and I grabbed that old cornet. And it was all beat up, there was about six holes in it. I found a barrel of coal tar, the stuff they use to work on the highway, and I took that coal tar and patched up the holes on the cornet. And my first song was "Jingle Bells." I was about seven. I started playing backwards. I was playing left-handed, man, 'cause nobody didn't know, my brother was gone, my daddy and ma didn't know no better, they didn't know shit, really, and my daddy used to fuss at me, *"Va la en dehors avec tout ça"*—"Go in the fields with all that noise!" *"Tous les blancs"*— "You gonna wake up all the white folks, they don't want to hear that noise. Get out of here with all that noise." And I had to go out in the woods, Jack, to the f——ing cotton fields to practice my cornet. I ain't know what I was blowing. I knew I could blow "Jingle Bells."

I kept on going, but I couldn't blow at home. Around sunset, my daddy came home from work, he took his bath after working hard in the fields, I had to respect him. So to play my horn I had to go about two or three miles from the house. But I loved it, I knew it was something that Jesus wanted me to do. And at that age I used to walk down the country roads and talk to God, I ain't even knew what God was about, but just asking, "Help me with this, protect me with this, I wanna be this one day when I grow up." And that's what I'm still doing now, blowing the trumpet, and talking to God.

I went back home one afternoon, and my dad was watching the news, I'll never forget, my mother had made a fricassée that day, brother, she had made a fricassée with some pork, pork ribs and pork tails, and pig feet in the fricassée. And I was eating my dinner, man, and my daddy looked at me and said, *"La musique, ce n'est pas rien du tout."* He said, "With that old horn you ain't gonna be nothing at all, you need to go to school, learn what you can do and go get you a job like everybody else." So at that age, man, what the hell I need with a job, you dig? You know, here I am, man, seven years old, just turning eight, I'm a stone country boy, saying, *"Oh, mais yeah, oh, mais non, cher, oh, mais,* I don't know, me." You know, I'm still talking like that, dig? But I kept cool with my dad with a positive attitude.

So I was in the elementary school band, playing cornet, but playing it backwards, brother, I'm playing it left-handed. So my band teacher came up to me and said, "Who taught you to play, who showed you that?" I said, "Me." Said, "My daddy wouldn't let me play the horn around the house so I went to the cotton fields and taught myself." He said, "You're good, but one thing, son, you're playing it wrong. If you going to be a horn player, you can't do it that way." After that we got a new band teacher, Alfred Ray Guillory from out of Plaisance, that's the little town where they have the zydeco festival now. He showed me how to switch from playing left-hand to playing right-handed. So I did, and you know what happened? He gave me a horn, brother. He gave me a school horn, a trumpet, he got tired of seeing me with that old beat-up, patched-up, coal-tarred cornet. I could read, you put some music in front of me, I could read. By then I was like twelve years old. So I kept on going, playing high school bands and summer programs and all, and I was getting real good at it. I was even playing clubs with Guitar Gable, Gabriel Perrodin, he gave me my first job.

Guitar Gable was one of the great talents of swamp pop. His records were successful on a regional level only, but their impact in Louisiana remains undiminished. Perrodin's hits, such as "Irene," are still prominent in the repertoire of many swamp pop, blues, and zydeco bands. He was coaxed out of retirement in the mid-nineties by rock/swamp pop guitarist C. C. Adcock, and still performs

on occasion. For Ceasar, working with Perrodin would be the first of many stints in the bands of noted performers.

That gig with Guitar Gable happened through Alfred Ray Guillory. He brung me on the gig one night, they needed a horn section, he was playing sax with them, making a little side change, so he brung me along. Yeah, I was twelve years old but I could hold my part. I couldn't hit no high C's, no high D's, I couldn't even solo, I didn't know what a solo was. But I could hold my part, Jack. So he got me in there, and I got to know Guitar Gable and all these guys from out of Opelousas. I was twelve years old, and skinny like a zydeco, like a snap bean, working with Guitar Gable.

My old man didn't like it. First of all, I had to hitchhike to get to town, 'cause I lived out in the country, way out from Basile, at least thirteen miles from town. But I kept gigging with the guy, Alfred Ray Guillory, my band teacher, he was helping me out, he was writing out the horn charts for us, and I could pick up the horn, play my piece. Playing those nightclubs. I was going to school with forty dollars in my pocket, Jack. Hey, I was rich, back in them days, no kids would ever come to school with that kind of money. And I always got my clothes from a black company called Eleganza. You know, I was one of those real sweet guys, a ladies' man, but I'm cool now that I'm married.

Then after I graduated, I got my diploma and hauled ass to Houston. My grandfather died, I stayed for his funeral, and after we buried him I left for Houston. Where else can

Warren Ceasar plays his trumpet out in the fields

you go when you're from the country? And I ended up playing with Isaac Hayes and Luther Ingram.

But when I hit Houston at first, it was *rough.* I'm starving, Jack. This dude had promised me a job, promised me this, promised me that, now I'm learning, I'm still a country boy still talking, *"Oh, mais yeah cher, oh, mais non."* But I can't go back home 'cause I got to prove a point to my old man. Then my brother who played the cornet, he moved to Houston from St. Louis, saved my ass, we got a place together. And I got a little gig playing with a guy named Lionel, Lionel, oh, shit, Lionel somebody — I can't remember now, it'll come to me. Twenty bucks a night. Hey, it was better than nothing, now I'm working three and four nights a week. So that kept on going for awhile, by now it's 1973, and this guy named Sammy Relford comes to the club and comes on to us like he's big time. Says he's talked to a producer from Stax Records, out of Memphis, Tennessee, and this dude at Stax is really interested in our band.

So like a bunch of monkeys, we gonna believe Sammy. We said, "Hey, man, these cats at Stax want us to come up there, let's go to Memphis." So we went. We all jumped in a truck, we all packed up, man, we had three female singers, three horns, a rhythm section, plus Sammy Relford. He told us that the shit was all set up. I done quit everything I had going, even left my brother behind, he's bitching at me, "Hey, man, you going to starve on that road, bro, I know what I'm talking about, I been out there."

So we get to Memphis, Jack, we get to Stax Records, and guess what? They don't know who the f—— we are. They don't know that we're coming up there, they don't know nothin' about it. It was all bullshit. I said, "Oh, Lord have mercy, my brother told me so. Now what I'm gonna do? I can't go back home and be the laughingstock of the whole family." So we hung around, man, for about six hours that day at Stax Records. They let us hang out in the yard, it was a fenced-in yard. And we met a guy named Luther Ingram. He had a big hit record, "If Loving You Is Wrong I Don't Want to Be Right," and he was looking for a band.

Luther let us in the building. We went in and sat in Studio B, and we started playing, man, started jamming. Luther said, "I want the three horn players, and I want the three girl singers, and I don't want nobody else." He put out the front money, bought all the equipment, uniforms, paid for hotel rooms, and we practiced. Isaac Hayes was on the tour, too. Okay, check this out. We got to Memphis on a Monday, by Wednesday we were rehearsing with Luther, that Friday morning we left Memphis, Jack, and drove to Houston, to play at the Pavilion. I'm back in Houston, at the Houston Pavilion, working with Luther Ingram and jamming with "the black Moses," Isaac Hayes. And I did that for about eleven months. Isaac Hayes used to call me "Country Ceasar."

You wanna know what they were they like to work for? It was hell. It was the underworld. I learned about convicts, I learned about prostitutes, I learned about dope, faggots, pimps, whores, bitches, you name it, Jack. Everything there was to know, right there, brother. Everything I learned, in high school, from my daddy and mama, my big brother, my band teachers — nobody could teach me nothin'. But out there I learned. So after eleven months I was in Dallas, Texas. I had toured all over America with these people, I did my thing, I made money, too, made sixty bucks a night. Back in them days, that was big money. So after eleven months of that I quit, in Dallas. Caught a ride back home with them same girls, they were called the Spark Sisters, out of Houston, some pretty black girls, and they could sing, *goddam*, they could sing. And this guy Sammy Relford was their uncle, the one who conned us into coming out on the road behind all that wild bullshit. But after eleven months I had enough of the Isaac Hayes Movement. It was too much for me, Jack. I came back to Houston and stayed there for three months and couldn't handle Houston no more. So I came back to Basile.

Then I got a job at Southwestern Foods in Lafayette. I didn't play music for a whole f——ing year, brother, 'cause I had got married and my wife she wanted me out of it. But music is like a drug, man. Got it in you, you gonna go for it. So I started playing trumpet with Major Handy, he was playing rock then, before he got into zydeco. This is the mid-1970s I'm talking about, there wasn't no whole lot of zydeco gigs, it was Top 40, soul, rock, a little blues. I was scuffling, and I had some problems, I got in some trouble. Went through a lot of crap, stayed in trouble for over a year. And then one day, I ran into L'il Bob, you know, from L'il Bob and the Lollipops. That's when things started getting good again.

L'il Bob, whose real name is Camille Bob, occupies a rather unique niche in swamp pop. A singing drummer (and Clifton Chenier's second cousin), he led a popular band called L'il Bob and the Lollipops during the 1950s and 1960s. Many Lafayette residents recall that L'il Bob played at their high school prom. The group still performs on occasion. Bob is also a songwriter, and one of his tunes, "I Got Loaded," was covered by Los Lobos on the group's acclaimed debut album *Will the Wolf Survive?* In 1979 Bob hired Warren Ceasar. Ceasar recalls:

I start blowing trumpet with L'il Bob, and playing flute, too. We recorded "Memphis Underground," that flute instrumental by Herbie Mann. And then one night right around 1980 I was talking on a pay phone in Lafayette, and you know who walked up to use the phone? Clifton Chenier. I had met him before, somewhere on the scene, one of the clubs. He asked me, "What you doing tonight?" I said, "I ain't doin' nothing." He said, "Bring your horn, bring your horn, come on over to the Grant Street Dance Hall." I went over there, walked in the club, and I went straight to the bandstand. I got on stage and took out my trumpet. Clifton's son C. J. was blowing his saxophone, that's before he switched over to the accordion. I started hitting these high D's and high C's, holding these high notes and Clifton's saying, "Hey, I like it." So we got to jamming—that's when me and C. J. got tight, you know, we became very good friends. I did a whole set that night. I told Clifton, "Hey, thank you, I appreciate it," I didn't get paid a penny, went on home.

Two weeks later, me and Clifton meet up again at the same pay phone. He said, "What you been doing?" He said, "Oh, that was nice, what you did for me the other night, yeah." He said, "Oh, but you blow some good horn, yeah, why don't you come meet us, we playin' Saturday night at the Dauphine Club, in Parks." That's when it all started, bro. That first night was at the Dauphine, way out in the country, that's when the shit hit the fan, Jack. That's what started everything with me and Clifton.

When I got into the band, this was right after Clifton had been real sick. He had half of his foot amputated, because of the diabetes. He was down, Jack, a lot of his musicians had quit him, some of 'em he had run off. But Robert St. Julian was still there, his drummer, and C. J., and Cliff's brother, Cleveland, playing scrubboard.

What I learned from Clifton was the best. To learn anything more, I had to go out on my own and front my own band. Yeah, Clifton taught me it all. We even had a fight coming out of Columbus, Ohio, on the way to Detroit. He pulled a gun on me, we got into one of the biggest fights ever—which caused us to become the best friends that was ever on this earth. I had to prove to the cat, "Hey, I'm a man, too, you dig, I'm working for you but I'm not your slave." Which is one thing that Clifton did bad sometimes, he would act like "Hey, I'm Clifton Chenier, you all do what I say or get the f——out."

We did a session in Chicago for Alligator Records, after Clifton had won the Grammy. Clifton got mad at the dude from Alligator, Bruce Iglauer, he was producing, and him and Cliff they couldn't agree about the music. Clifton said, "F——it!" and pulled out a big wad of cash, and he just bought the master tapes, peeled off about twelve hundred dollars, took the tapes and walked out with them. That's how they settled that disagreement. It was funny to me. I witnessed the whole thing. Bruce is a good guy. He was upset, he said, "What should I do?" I said, "Leave it alone, brother, ain't nothing you can do now, once Clifton Chenier gets pissed off you just leave him alone, Jack."

I'll tell you something, I never ever thought nobody was going to hire me to play no trumpet in a zydeco band. But Clifton was a good teacher, man. Through the years, Clifton and I got real, real close. I hate to say it but we got closer than me and my own father ever did. See, Clifton became more than just a friend to me, he was more like a father. Even with problems in my marriage, Clifton talked a lot about that, about how him and his wife, Margaret, had stuck with it, worked it out. I was offered a lot of gigs when Clifton got sick and had to start cancelling some of his shows, but I turned them all down. I couldn't do that. Clifton Chenier meant too much to me.

You know, Isaac Hayes and them taught me all about the streets, the underworld. But what Clifton taught me was how to be a *man*.

Urbane
Zydeco

**Lynn August:
"I Like a Challenge"**

Accordionist Lynn August has followed a career path that is similar to Warren Ceasar's in terms of varied experience yet is quite different because of August's deliberate, studious nature. But this methodical approach does not make August's brand of zydeco any less soulful or convincing. Without such self-discipline, in fact, he could not have taken on the piano accordion as a new instrument, mastered it quickly, and then returned to the Creole roots of his childhood.

I was born in 1948, in Lafayette. I had an uncle that would play zydeco accordion, mostly for fun, his name was Claudel Duffy. But where I really got my influence for music was from my parents. Back in the fifties there was very little to offer for blind people as far as a livelihood. I've been blind since birth, and my mother heard of a blind musician who was actually earning a good living. He was going under the name of R. C. Robinson, and later he changed it to Ray Charles. He played in Lafayette in the early fiftiess, my parents went to see him, and right away they got me started. They bought me a phonograph and some records by Fats Domino, Chuck Willis, and Johnny Ace. They were always very supportive of me being a musician.

In the mid-fifties the guitar got real popular because of Chuck Berry and Elvis Presley. Just about every other kid on my block had a guitar. My cousins had a little neighborhood band with guitars, and I'd sit on one of these great big number three washtubs, turn it upside down and beat on it — I was their drummer. I finally graduated to get my own drum set, at age eight, and by the time I was ten, I was playing in a real band. Drums was my first instrument.

I started gigging at a place called the Peppermint Lounge, six nights a week, with a piano player named Olin Boudreaux, he went by the name of Rollin' Dice. People often suggested that I should switch to keyboards but I kept playing drums for awhile, with a guy out of Lafayette named Jay Nelson. He had a record out called "Baby Please," a rhythm and blues type thing, and we'd work on shows with rhythm and blues guys like Ernie K-Doe, out of New Orleans. He had a big hit then with "Mother-in-Law."

Around 1963 I made the switch and decided to start my own band. I was practicing, learning the keyboards, and still playing drums in another little combo with Buckwheat playing organ. Buckwheat left so I took over on keyboards and hired someone else as the drummer.

At that time the only person who really played a lot of zydeco was Clifton Chenier, it wasn't really that popular then. I got to know Clifton later, but I used to hear his music all the time, because I grew up right across the street from a lounge where the jukebox would play Cliff and Fats Domino all day long, and they had a loudspeaker that played it outside, too. I learned to sing "Paper in My Shoe," Cliff's version, not the one by Boozoo Chavis.

Marcel Dugas

In 1964, I switched to organ, that's when the Hammond B-3 organ came out. I dropped the band and started working as a solo organist, four nights a week, for three hundred dollars, big money back then. The club was over in St. Martinville, twenty miles out of Lafayette, Beno's Lounge. There are a bunch of zydeco clubs out there now. I would mix

up the music, do a lot of Stevie Wonder songs, some country music, some jazz. It was a white club. Eventually I hired a drummer and I called us the Lynn August Duo. We'd play four nights at Beno's and we'd double up on Fridays and Saturdays, playing other gigs, and then I had *another* gig besides that on Sunday, starting at midnight and going til 5 A.M. on Monday morning. There was no closing time to worry about back then.

In sixty-seven I formed a seven-piece soul band with a horn section. We'd travel around Texas and Louisiana, play Otis Redding songs, all of the Motown stuff, Stax hits by Sam and Dave, Eddie Floyd, Rufus Thomas. And we'd do a lot of New Orleans R&B, Fats Domino, Smiley Lewis. I had that big band 'til 1969, cut it down to four pieces, worked that 'til about 1971, and then I went back to playing my B-3, solo, with a drum machine. I worked the hotel lounge circuit, traveling all around the country. I was by myself, that's when I got my first guide dog. I would hire people to drive me to the next town and then I would stay right at the hotel where I was playing. The gig would last for about a month at a time. I didn't really have any living expenses, sometimes I had two, three, four, five checks backed up. I took correspondence courses and learned to read and write music by braille, and I took some music theory, too.

By 1977 I got tired of doing that, and I got my first zydeco gig. I went on the road with Marcel Dugas. He had played accordion and I played organ. Marcel played basically the same style as Clifton Chenier, and Clifton Chenier had expanded his band by hiring Buckwheat to play organ, so Marcel followed suit. I had always kept up with my French, so I understood everything that was going on. I worked with Marcel and I got to like zydeco music. Of course, I like a lot of different variations of it, but this particular style that he had, he could be bluesy, he could be French, and he could be high energy. And that's what had captured me.

I started thinking about forming my own zydeco band, but only if I could lead it and play the accordion. I've always been a bandleader, I guess that's the Leo in me. I want to make all the decisions. But I was getting into my thirties and I didn't know if I wanted to learn a new instrument. I'm a bit of a perfectionist. If I can't do something right then I'm not gonna mess with it.

I guess my two other musical loves that I enjoyed playing, besides zydeco, are jazz and gospel music. I always played a lot of jazz on the Hammond B-3, and I kicked the bass pedals like all those great soul-jazz organ players, people like Brother Jack McDuff and Richard "Groove" Holmes. But I was really into the idea of zydeco, so I left Marcel Dugas with the goal of starting my own zydeco band.

But when you play for a living, you can't just say, "I'm only gonna play what I want." I went to work as a choir director for a couple of churches here in Lafayette, around 1979. One of them had a thirty-voice choir. I like a challenge, and I wanted to put my musical knowledge to work. It was great because I'd write different harmony parts for different sections, it was very satisfying. Plus I'd play the organ at restaurants, so I stayed busy and made a living, too.

Then in 1988 I produced my first album, *Party Time,* for Floyd Soileau. It was a total mixture: lounge music, swamp pop, country, rhythm and blues, and a couple of zydeco songs that I played with an effect on my keyboard that sounded just like an accordion. Floyd called me and said, "I been getting more compliments for the zydeco songs than any others on the album, and the radio stations have been playing them. You can sing in French and you got a good blues voice, you really ought to try zydeco."

I purchased my accordion in June of 1989. I went out and checked with Marc Savoy in Eunice. I had no idea that them things sell for three thousand dollars. I thought I'd pick up a used accordion for a couple of hundred. But my wife said, "Buy the good one, 'cause if you spend that kind of money then I know you're going to learn to play it." I took it home and I practiced, I must have put in fourteen hours a day. One day my little boy said, "Hey, Dad's getting good." I kept practicing. The keyboard side of the accordion was no problem, 'cause I already knew how to play keyboard. But it took awhile to learn exactly where each button was on the other side.

With zydeco I can play for an audience, and still play something I like. When I was in the lounge business, I had to play songs I didn't really care for, but that's the songs that are selling. But really, I can't think of a single thing I don't like by Clifton Chenier. I just enjoy what I'm doing. And I take careful consideration in all the musicians I have with me. I sit everybody down and say, "Look, it's not how many notes you play, because a lot of zydeco is basically pattern music, the same thing over and over again. Now, if you're

Marc Savoy in his workshop fabricating a handmade "Acadian" brand accordion

going out there to run the scales, play all the drum rudiments, and show off, then you're on the wrong gig." Because when zydeco first came about, it was just the accordion and the scrubboard, the *frottoir*. And even before that people used to just sing, the old *juré* singing. I'm going to put a *juré* song on my next album. I used to hear *juré* singing when I grew up. My grandfather had grown up out in the country, and he'd sing some of the *juré* songs that he heard out there. I was practicing that *juré* one day and my mama walked in, said, "My goodness," said, "Where'd you get that from?" She said, "That reminds me of the old-time house dances."

I want to say that my grandfather was a big, big inspiration to me because a blind people's worst enemies are the people who'll baby you. You won't learn to take care of yourself, you never learn to be nothing. My grandfather would brag all over, "I got a grandson that's blind but he can do anything he wants." And he started me on my attitude that I can do anything. I know how to build, I did about 70 percent of the work on my house.

I have a lot of plans for what I'm going to be doing in the future. What I want to do is keep my zydeco plain and simple. And if I go back to some other style I'm gonna put down my accordion, get back on a regular keyboard, and do it right.

The **Contemporary** Spectrum

"There's Room for Us All"

Wilbert Guillory's description of the Zydeco Festival as a "family reunion" underscores the importance of lineage in Creole music. The personnel list of many zydeco bands could almost double as a genealogical chart. These pedigrees include the Ardoin, Broussard, Carrier, Chavis, Chenier, Frank, Prudhomme, and Williams clans, and the Creole cowboys known as Delafose. The Delafose saga is a microcosm of zydeco's development during the 1980s and 1990s and its prospects for the new millenium.

From the mid-1970s until his death in 1994, accordionist John Delafose led a popular zydeco band called the Eunice Playboys. As seen in the feature film *Passion Fish*, he was a powerful instigator of dance floor fervor. Delafose's popularity surged in 1980 with a regional hit entitled "Joe Pitre a deux femmes" ("Joe Pitre Got Two Women"). The song was first recorded by Bois-sec Ardoin and Canray Fontenot, and its revival by John Delafose had far-reaching effects.

"I started out playing on an old white piano accordion, because that's what Clifton Chenier had," Jeffery Broussard told Michael Tisserand. The son of rural stylist Delton Broussard, Jeffery was a founding member of a funk-influenced band called Zydeco Force; the group formed in the late 1980s and was quite popular during the following decade. "But when Delafose was playing that little single thing," Broussard continued, "they were going crazy over that. I started playing that, then I wouldn't give it up for nothing in the world. 'Joe Pitre,' that brought the single-note accordion back." In bringing back the single-row accordion, "Joe Pitre a deux femmes" encouraged the return of single-note stylists such as Boozoo Chavis. There were broader ramifications as well, because the song became popular just as an ascendant genre known as rap was gaining airplay on black radio around America.

Commercial stations in Creole country followed suit, and zydeco remained relegated to weekend programming, for the most part. Despite some obvious differences, many rap songs had striking if coincidental similarities to the rural zydeco sound of "Joe Pitre a deux femmes." Both consisted of repeated riffs and vocal refrains with little emphasis on melodic lines, chord changes, or harmonic resolution. Both succeeded musically because of catchy riffs—

known as "hooks" to record producers—and rhythmic grooves that inspired dancing, albeit to quite different steps. Listeners and musicians began to sense a connection between the two, lending critical mass to the emergence of a stylistic hybrid. The unlikely result was that John Delafose and the first-generation rappers influenced zydeco by converging on it from opposite poles. It's safe to assume that no one in either camp dreamt that their unintentional synthesis would set the stage for today's dominant trend: zydeco nouveau.

Zydeco nouveau has many critics. Some oppose it from a purist perspective, citing the dominance of English lyrics, while others are alarmed by its typically low standards of musical craft. But even these detractors would have to acknowledge that zydeco nouveau is vastly popular. This is the sound that draws the largest crowds of young Creoles to the dance halls and has made zydeco a viable option for the greatest number of musicians. Nouveau has its own pantheon, including Keith Frank, Step Rideau, J. Paul, Jr., Beau Jocque, Rosie Ledet, L'il Malcolm Walker, and Chris Ardoin. Only Beau Jocque can boast of significant mainstream recognition; his primal, growling voice and imposing stage presence have graced millions of households thanks to television hosts David

Keith Frank (center) at Richard's Club

Letterman and Conan O'Brien. But all of these artists are important figures on the dance hall and trail ride circuit. They command loyal followings, and have become embroiled in some fierce rivalries.

Like many musical terms, "zydeco nouveau" has rather arbitrary guidelines. Zydeco Force is often credited as founding the nouveau movement, for instance, but the term and the band were never contemporaneous. There is also considerable stylistic range among the current artists. Beau Jocque explores seventies funk, and reprises the classic interplay of James Brown and Bobby Byrd in his stage-patter dialogue with drummer Steve Charlot. Chris Ardoin plays waltzes such as "Bonsoir Moreau" that have bloomed on his family tree for at least four generations. L'il Malcolm Walker and Rosie Ledet both have rich voices with great potential for "black contemporary" commercial crossover. But the various forms of zydeco nouveau do have traits in common, especially in the booming bass lines that are locked in with a prevalent drum beat called the "double kick." These features reflect the obvious influence of rap and hip-hop, as does the use of rap's staccato, declamatory vocals. Full-throated singing also flourishes, however, and since rap and hip-hop do not use accordions or make references to trail rides, the nouveau sound still maintains a strong regional identity.

The penchant for minimalism in zydeco nouveau can be heard in the lyrics to songs such as J. Paul, Jr.'s "Bad by Myself." In the rendition on his album, *Taking Over*, these lines are repeated four times, and occasional ad-libbed shouts are the only other words:

> I can do bad by myself, I can do bad by myself, I can do bad
> myself
> I don't need your help,
> I can do bad by myself, I can do bad by myself, I can do bad
> myself
> I don't need your help
> I'd rather be alone

In theory this pattern seems excruciating, but the double kick and a lilting accordion figure make it quite danceable. Some nouveau lyrics are even more basic and simply repeat the song's title, as heard on numerous renditions of "Pop That Coochie." Single-row accordions can easily fill the rudimentary demands of zydeco nouveau, and, while the single-row is not inherently simplistic, only a few accomplished soloists have emerged from the nouveau school. Significantly, most of them play the piano accordion. Soloing is further diminished by the fact that zydeco nouveau bands rarely include a saxophonist, although electric guitarists do get ample time to "stretch out." Many employ a frantic, intense style reminiscent of heavy metal rock.

Although the nouveau school may prove to be a passing fad, it has generated some contemporary classics, including Beau Jocque's rousing "Give Him Cornbread" and Chris Ardoin's none-too-subtle "Lick It Up." These songs are apt to remain popular for years to come. But the success of zydeco nouveau has also sparked a lively debate over such issues as the artistic health of zydeco, the integrity of its future, and the specter of assimilation. "Today's zydeco is lyrically impoverished," Barry Ancelet commented with obvious disappointment, while C. J. Chenier stated, "I don't want that zyde-rap sound. They play a riff, they shout a couple of words, and that's it."

Rap is a major force within the music industry and an important expressive vehicle within the African-American community. Nevertheless, many black musicians who play other styles have extremely negative attitudes towards it. Their objections, like those of many whites, focus on the violence and misogyny of some rap lyrics, with added concerns over the negative racial stereotypes that are reinforced. Another complaint is the marginal musicianship often found in rap, which sends a message to young players that success need not be based on hard work and practice. "Rap is nothing but noise," according to New Orleans R&B guitarist Snooks Eaglin. Leroy "Sugarfoot" Bonner, guitarist and vocalist with the seventies funk band the Ohio Players, was more explicit: "There's no such thing as rap music. There's just rap—there's no *music* involved in it at all. *Music* has melody, lyrics, and content."

Yet some researchers who revere zydeco's most traditional forms also support zydeco nouveau, rap influences and all. "Zydeco nouveau is a style appropriate to this period in the evolution of Creole culture," Nick Spitzer stated. "While it has not developed much in terms of lyrics or instrumental soloing, it is often more rhythmically powerful and complex than Creole dance music that came before. And, unlike the earlier forms of zydeco, it has been much more persuasive in terms of getting a new young generation of Creoles into the community dance halls. If you apply the same argument about lyrical simplicity to the relationship of country music—which is a lyric-focused form—with rock and roll—which is a rhythm-oriented form—you end up denying the undeniable, which is rock's power to move people. Besides, zydeco nouveau continues the traditional symbolic focus on the Creole bandleader/singer/accordionist as kingly protagonist."

When I interviewed Clifton Chenier in 1983, the scathing remarks that he made about disco music ring equally true about today's rap-inspired zydeco:

People used to laugh at me for playing the accordion. People used to hate to see an accordion, but now, man, look at 'em! Everybody want to grab an accordion, now, man, *everybody!* They learn one key and they go on with it, sometimes I just laugh, me, but I don't say nothin', I just laugh, man, you know everybody tryin' to make it.

See in the 1940s, '50s, up to the '60s, that was music. That was really music, but when it started gettin' later than that, well, drums was all that was goin' on, "shika-boom, shika-boom." But in the 1940s, the '50s, man, they had *bands* out here, real bands, oh, yeah. Now you take like a good friend of mine, B. B. King, I been knowin' B. B. since 1947, and—*pay attention*—every record he make is about something that happened to somebody. A true story.

But now what you gettin' these days, what you gettin'? You ain't gettin' nothin', no, you ain't, just noise and jumpin' up and down! In 1949 and '50, the '60s, them people was dancin', that's what you would call it, dancin'. But what they got now, man, disco and all that, that's all right for the youngsters, that's what they like, you know, but in my book, it don't show me nothin'.

Ever the canny pragmatist, Chenier managed to stifle his revulsion long enough to include an instrumental called "Zydeco Disco" on his Grammy-winning album *I'm Here!* Perhaps he thought the title would help sales, although the song had little in common with disco music. There were no swirling string arrangements or pulsing bass drums, and a more accurate name would have been "Zydeco Funk." While disco never influenced zydeco to the same degree that rap has, Chenier made an astute point that prophetically applies to current concerns about "lyrical impoverishment":

I like to hear something with ideas, you know, give me an idea of something. Maybe your wife done walked off and left you. Why she left you? That's the point, why she left you? You did something you ain't had no business doing, or maybe *she* was wrong, but *something happened.*

See, a lot of people don't understand that. They make a little record and go on with it, but they don't tell a story, and you know why? They ain't got no story to tell you, 'cause they ain't been through nothin', they ain't been nowhere yet. You got to go through the mill for that, now you catch fellas like me, fellas like B. B. King, Big Joe Turner, Fats Domino, them fellas can *tell you something,* that's right, they can sit down and tell you something, 'cause they've been out there. You never learn nothin' 'til you go through the mill. Like me, see, I had to go through all of that, to be a musician.

Disco's all right, it's all right, you know them kids like it, it's good, and I like to listen to some of it myself, but it ain't showin' me nothin'. When you really want to listen to music, you got to go back there, man, back there in the fifties, sixties, when there were *musicians.* Chuck Berry, Little Walter in Chicago with the harmonica, men like Willie Dixon, Muddy Waters, they got a story behind every record they made, you know. That kind of music, that's when you're sitting down at home, you're lonesome, thinking about some of your old friends from way back, you put one of their records on and you hear them telling you somethin'. You put one of these new records on, what you got? "Shika-boom, shika-boom."

Zydeco nouveau's practitioners are well aware of such criticism. Although the issue of lyrical pablum has not been directly addressed, they staunchly defend the sonic aspects of their style. Accordionist Keith Frank told Michael Tisserand that "I get criticized because I don't play a lot of waltzes. I know a thousand waltzes, but I just don't like to play them." Ironically, Keith Frank emerged during the 1980s from his father's group, Preston Frank and the Family Band. This was one of the last rural zydeco groups to feature a fiddler, and Keith Frank learned many waltzes during his apprenticeship—but even if he did enjoy playing them, his current following would probably not.

Some nouveau artists create substantial music, and make an articulate case in support of their work. L'il Brian Terry in particular has forged an effective and melodic blend of zydeco, rap, funk, and soul. This is evidenced by his challenging arrangements, rich harmonies, and piano accordion finesse. Terry's suc-

Roy "Chubby" Carrier, Jr., during a videotaping

Roy Carrier at his nightclub, the Offshore Lounge, Lawtell, Louisiana

cessful synthesis of contemporary styles follows squarely in the parameter-expanding footsteps of Clifton Chenier and Stanley "Buckwheat" Dural. "I was raised with zydeco," Terry told Michael Tisserand. "Zydeco was practically a meal at my table. But, you know, I'm a young man, and I started liking Snoop Doggy Dogg rap, and Tupac. So I started to feel, if they can do it, man, why can't I do it—but just do it with zydeco music, something I was brought up with?"

Although accordionist Terrance Simien emerged a generation before zydeco nouveau, he has also been criticized for a repertoire that wanders far afield from tradition. So has Simien's neighbor and colleague, accordionist Chubby Carrier, who learned his craft at his father's club, the Offshore Lounge in Lawtell. The music of Chubby Carrier and Terrance Simien is more complex than that played by most nouveau stylists, delving into rock, funk, reggae, and New Orleans R&B. Simien's sound reflects the strong influence of the Neville Brothers, especially Aaron Neville's vocal style. As he explained, Simien sees such diversity as an organic process:

I was born in 1965, and raised in Mallet. That's a little rural community, near Opelousas. My first instrument was the trumpet, in the school band, from fourth grade through tenth. We played some classical things. I can read music, and I still like Bach and Beethoven a

Terrance Simien near his home in Mallet, Louisiana

lot. As far as popular styles, for a while I only liked soul music, but then I got into the Beatles, Bob Dylan, and things like the sound track to *Star Wars*—I loved that.

When I was a teenager, in the late seventies, early eighties, there was a zydeco dance every Friday night at our church, St. Ann's in Mallet. People like Delton Broussard and Nolton Semien [no relation] would play traditional zydeco. That inspired me. You know, when you go to dances when you're around fourteen or fifteen years old, out with your parents, and you fall in love, meet your first girlfriend — that's a special time.

Besides going to those church dances I went to Slim's and Richard's. People like John Delafose would play and he'd tear it up with that "Joe Pitre." I listened to the radio a lot, too. There are lots of zydeco shows on Saturday morning, and I heard Clifton, Buckwheat, Rockin' Dopsie. John Delafose. I started teaching myself accordion, and I played my first dance when I was seventeen. It was hard work playing those dances around home, at Richard's or Slim's Y-Ki-Ki, though now that we're traveling all the time, I do miss it. We play almost all white clubs now, the money is better. Those people at home are your biggest critics. If they like you, they'll let you know, but if they don't, they tell you that, too, and they're not always very nice about it.

Terrance Simien and the Mallet Playboys entered the national arena through a role in *The Big Easy*. This was arranged by Dickie Landry, whose connections had also led to Rockin' Dopsie's work with Paul Simon. Simien and the band appeared both in the film and on the sound track album. When *The Big Easy* was released in 1987, they embarked on a life of constant touring, which continues on a dozen years later. Simien often sings in French and is well versed in traditional zydeco. But he thrives on variety, and such eclectic taste has frustrated producers who seek to channel Simien's talent. Simien sought to explain his position both in interviews and with a 1993 album entitled *There's Room for Us All*.

I respect all music that's being made, and I know that it takes a lot of love to just keep playing folk music, traditional music. I think it's great when people do it the old way, like it was a hundred years ago. But I also don't feel that anyone has a right to say what is or isn't zydeco. It don't have to be played one certain way.

These purists shouldn't knock other people who are trying to modernize the music and project their own way of feeling. Buckwheat got criticized for not playing real zydeco—well, he was playing eighties zydeco when he broke out and made his name, and it was good music. Hell, if we all play the same damn way, what's gonna happen? Everyone's gonna sound the same.

I feel very lucky about the way things are going. We have a long ways to go before we

Germaine Jack

can sit down, though. The onliest thing I want out of zydeco is to be able to play music, and not have no one or nothing deny me from it. If I can have that for the rest of my life—well, that's it.

Change was swirling around zydeco by the late 1980s, and John Delafose could not have been less interested. He kept on working at Richard's, Slim's Y-Ki-Ki, and the Maple Leaf in New Orleans, maintaining his unvarnished, rural style. Delafose featured two of his sons in the band; Tony alternated between bass and *frottoir,* while Geno functioned as both the drummer and the accordion understudy. When John took a break, Geno played accordion, and his cousin, Germaine Jack, would lay down his *frottoir* and move over to the drums. This family game of musical chairs was expanded by the presence of the Prudhomme brothers, Charles and Joseph, on guitar and bass. Inspired by his siblings' work with the Delafoses, a third brother—Willis Prudhomme— emerged in the mid-1980s as a popular zydeco accordionist whose style bore the distinct imprint of both John Delafose and Cajun traditionalist Nathan Abshire.

John Delafose had a similarly "all in the family" approach towards his choice of his material. Like traditional musicians in many genres, Delafose drew on a deep repertoire of self-proclaimed "originals." In truth these "compositions" assembled fragments from innumerable other songs that themselves were formed in the same piecemeal manner. This continued recycling reveals that the folkloric process and oral tradition are still thriving in zydeco. The ongoing interchange of ideas, some of which have archaic roots, is fascinating to watch in progress. But it also creates legal

nightmares in terms of establishing the authorship of songs, securing copyrights for them, and collecting song-publishing royalties. Substantiating such a claim may well be worth extensive effort and expense, since legal ownership of just one successful song can bring lifetime financial security.

Not surprisingly, these claims generate heated disputes among musicians, songwriters, and music publishers. Folk-rooted genres such as zydeco, Cajun music, blues, rockabilly, and bluegrass are especially prone to such controversy, and are overpopulated with people whose obstinate mantra is "I wrote that!" Some people really believe that they did, while others are unabashed opportunists who shrewdly figure that their claims will stand unchallenged. Instead of "wrote," the appropriate verbs are often "borrowed" or "stole."

L'il Brian Terry at Dockside Studios, Maurice, Louisiana

These complexities are illustrated by a look at the songs on *Père et Garçon Zydeco*, a 1992 album that cofeatured John and Geno Delafose. (In standard French, *"père et garçon"* translates into "father and boy"; in Louisiana idiomatic usage, it means "father and son.") The first number, "Ma coeur fait mal" ("My Heart Aches"), was based on "Fi fi foncho," a two-step popularized by Nathan Abshire in the 1950s. On the heels of the Boozoo Chavis hit "Dog Hill" came a canine romp entitled "Watch That Dog." "That dog might be anything, or any one," Geno admonished. "Your friends, your enemies, your boss, your old lady...You got to watch them." The two-step "Down in Texas Way" used the melody to Dewey Balfa's "Quand j'étais pauvre" ("When I Was Poor")—although, as on "Ma coeur fait mal," John Delafose changed the song by dispensing with its bridge. The title track,"Père et Garçon Zydeco," paid homage to Clifton Chenier's rendition of "Zydeco sont pas salés."

"I Can't Stop Lovin' You" was John Delafose's loose interpretation of a Don Gibson country hit that was also successful for Ray Charles. "We dig country music," John Delafose explained. "We listen to Dolly Parton quite a bit, Randy Travis, George Jones, all those guys. We get a lot of requests for country, especially in white clubs like the Maple Leaf in New Orleans." It was probably such requests that inspired John to write the free-form country tune "Go Back Where You Been," which he performed complete with a put-on twangy accent. There was also a connection to country music on "La misère m'a fait brailler" ("Misery Made Me Cry"), which used a tune based on Willis Prudhomme's "My Woman Is a Salty Dog." The ambiguous sexual term "salty dog" is the title of a popular bluegrass number recorded by Flatt and Scruggs, among many others. It also appears on numerous blues and jazz records dating back to the 1930s, by artists including Kokomo Arnold and New Orleans pianist Jelly Roll Morton.

John Delafose selected material from all over this multicultural map, and replenished the supply by contributing his own influential riffs and arrangements. The success of "Joe Pitre a deux femmes" prompted a series of follow-ups including "Joe Pitre Lost His Two Women" and "Joe Pitre Is Broke" by Delafose and other artists; Willis Prudhomme intensified the zydeco soap opera with "My Woman Slept in Joe Pete's Bed." Besides teaching his sons to play zydeco and giving inadvertent impetus to the nouveau movement, John

Left: Nathan Williams, Jr. with Sid "El Sid O" Williams, left, in doorway
and Nathan Williams at Sid's One—Stop, Lafayette, Louisiana
Above: Nathan Williams

Delafose directly inspired such accordionists as Prudhomme, Thomas "Big Hat" Fields and Miss Ann Goodly. As of this writing, Goodly is inactive, but during the early 1990s she was a regular at Slim's Y-Ki-Ki, Richard's, and her grandfather's club, Papa Paul's, in Mamou.

After falling ill on the bandstand at Richard's, John Delafose died in September of 1994. Under Geno's leadership, the Eunice Playboys eliminated such rough edges as "jumping time," while still maintaining a traditional aesthetic. Geno changed the band's name to French Rockin' Boogie, and it is currently one of the most exciting and diverse groups in zydeco, pleasing folk festival purists and dancing hedonists alike. Despite such creativity and national acclaim, Geno Delafose does not draw big crowds among the young Creoles who flock to hear zydeco nouveau—but, like his father, he has no interest in trends. "I get a lot of complaints from some of the young people," Delafose told Keith Spera of the New Orleans *Times-Picayune.* "They say, 'Oh, you play too many waltzes.' You know what? I'm happy people don't appreciate my music around here like they do elsewhere. I really enjoy the road, and I'm making a good living, and I'm not ready to be popular at home."

Accordionist Nathan Williams has much in common with Geno Delafose. Both are heritage-conscious modernists, born in the mid-1960s, who are more accomplished and eclectic than most of their zydeco nouveau contemporaries. Both maintain large followings on the international touring circuit. Like Geno Delafose and French Rockin' Boogie, the music of Nathan and the Zydeco Cha-Chas balances French and English lyrics and draws from a broad range of eras and styles. Williams writes many of his own songs, in a genre that can always use imaginative new material. His originals include "Everything on a Hog Is Good"—a bilingual tribute to Creole cuisine and thrifty home economics—and "If You Got a Problem." Williams's music also reflects the strong influence of Clifton Chenier. His first recording, a 45, was an adaptation of Chenier's "Sa m'appel fou" ("They Call Me Crazy"), and Chenier's repertoire is frequently mined by the Zydeco Cha-Chas. As Williams recounted, Clifton Chenier was his childhood idol:

I used to go hear Clifton when he played at the Casino Club in St. Martinville. That's where I was born, in 1963. But I didn't actually see Clifton *at* the club, 'cause I was too little to come in. One time I was watching Clifton by lookin' through the window from outside, standing on some boxes. The lady who ran the club, she didn't want us hanging around 'cause we were too young. They had one of them big windows, and one of them big old fans. I got too close and it cut off the bill of my hat! Oh, man, look, that old lady came and run us out of there, took our bicycles away and everything, but still I never stopped goin'.

When I got a little older, we moved to Lafayette. See, my oldest brother, Sid, he raised us after my father died, and he was like a father to the rest of us. We're a close family, all we really got is each other. One of my other brothers, Dennis, he plays guitar in my band. He's a really good painter, too, he shows his paintings at art galleries all over the country. And I got my first cousin Mark Williams playing the rubboard.

When I was little, Sid got hurt real bad working offshore. He got a nice insurance settlement, and he bought a grocery store, he called it Sid's One-Stop, in Lafayette. Buckwheat and my brother are old friends, and I used to go by Buckwheat's house. For awhile he was livin' right across the street from the store. He'd be sitting down playin' the accordion, and I'd go visit him all the time. Sometimes he'd call up and say, "Hey, bring me a six-pack," and we'd sit down and talk, and drink beer and play music.

At that time, I was in about tenth grade, sixteen or seventeen. I had seen Buckwheat before that, I used to go to his dances and he'd let me play a few songs, and that gave me the feeling for music. Then my brother Sid got me my first accordion. He's a whole lot of all this that's happening for me, a big part of my playing music. When I ain't had the money to buy an accordion he bought my first one for me. And when I started out his wife bought me my first equipment, two monitors, a mixing board, everything. At first I wasn't playing with a band, I was just practicing and getting things together, teaching myself and learning from Buckwheat. And I'm gonna tell you where I learned mostly, too—practicing back in the rest room here at the store. I'd come back here every five minutes, maybe stay ten minutes. Then Sid would come back and say, "Hey, man, we gotta take care of business." So Sid and my sister-in-law helped me out a lot and that meant a whole lot to me.

And Buckwheat always did take his time with me, too. Even if *People* magazine was there to photograph him or whatever, he'd have me get in the picture with him. You can't ask for better. People say I always talk about Buckwheat, but, hey, he helped me—they didn't help me. You gotta give a man credit where credit belong. If it weren't for Buckwheat you think I'd be with Rounder Records?

"Can I brag on Buckwheat, too?" Sidney Williams interrupted. "After we moved to Lafayette and I opened my store, I used to promote dances here and there. I had bought a vacant lot down the street to stop somebody else from building another store close to mine. Buckwheat told me, 'Man, you like to give dances, you should build you a club there.' So I did, and I named it El Sid O's Zydeco & Blues Club, after me. Buckwheat played there for our grand opening on Mother's Day, 1985, and Nathan plays there a lot when he's in town. You know, I'm proud of him and Buckwheat, both of them."

The modern setting of El Sid O's shows how effectively zydeco adapts to a variety of environments. Nathan and the Zydeco Cha-Chas perform at El Sid O's, as do zydeco old-timers such as Sampy and the Bad Habits and aspiring young artists, including Corey Arceneaux. On the blues side, singer Patrick Henry and his Liberation Band reprise the classics of Clarence Carter, Z. Z. Hill, Percy Sledge and Otis Redding, along with a touch of zydeco nouveau. A photo of Clifton Chenier presides over the happy dancers and rich musical mixture that fill the room.

If up-and-coming musicians continue to maintain this robust balance, then zydeco seems assured of a healthy future. No one can predict precisely what form that future will take, and assimilation is apt to make some inroads, as it did in the 1960s when zydeco almost died out. But the odds for zydeco's survival are much better now because of the international recognition that it has received. Some trendiness may be lost, but solid foundations will prevent a backslide into regional obscurity.

"The good Lord left me here for a purpose," Clifton Chenier sang on *I'm Here!*: "I brought the zydeco back, and it's back to stay." Today, Chenier's purpose surges forward as a vital, joyous work in progress. From sleek urban nightclubs to the next roadhouse in the cane fields, more great music awaits.

Gerard Delafose "sitting in" with John Delafose and the Eunice Playboys, c. 1990

Bibliography

Abrahams, Roger D. *Deep Down in the Jungle: Negro Narrative Folklore from the Streets of Philadelphia.* Chicago: Aldine Publishing, 1970.

Ancelet, Barry Jean. *The Makers of Cajun Music.* Photographs by Elemore Morgan, Jr. Austin: University of Texas Press, 1984; new edition, University Press of Mississippi, 1999 (the foreword is by Ralph Rinzler, and the title appears on the cover in French, also: *Musiciens cadiens et créoles*).

Ancelet, Barry Jean, Jay Edwards, and Glen Pitre. *Cajun Country.* Jackson: University Press of Mississippi, 1991.

Ancelet, Barry Jean, and Alan Lomax. *Louisiana Cajun and Creole Music. 1934: The Lomax Recordings.* Ville Platte, LA: Swallow Records, 1987 (an extensive booklet that accompanies a two-volume long-play album).

Barker, Danny. *A Life in Jazz.* Edited by Alyn Shipton. New York: Oxford University Press, 1986.

Bernard, Shane K. *Swamp Pop: Cajun and Creole Rhythm and Blues.* Jackson: University Press of Mississippi, 1996.

Berry, Jason, Jonathan Foose, and Tad Jones. *Up from the Cradle of Jazz: New Orleans Music Since World War II.* Athens: University of Georgia Press, 1986.

Brasseaux, Carl A. *The Founding of New Acadia: The Beginnings of Acadian Life in Louisiana, 1765–1803.* Baton Rouge: Louisiana State University Press, 1996.

———. *Acadian to Cajun: Transformation of a People, 1803–1877.* Jackson: University Press of Mississippi, 1992.

Broven, John *South to Louisiana: The Music of the Cajun Bayous.* Gretna, LA: Pelican Publishing, 1987.

Cable, George W. *The Dance in Place Congo: Creole Slave Songs.* New Orleans: Faruk von Turk, 1974.

Dorman, James H., ed. *Creoles of Color of the Gulf South.* Knoxville: University of Tennessee Press, 1996 (includes significant essays by Barry Ancelet and Nick Spitzer).

Drust, Greg. *Zydeco Dynamite: The Clifton Chenier Anthology.* Santa Monica, CA: Rhino Records, Inc., 1993 (an extensive booklet that accompanies a CD anthology).

Floyd, Samuel A., Jr. *The Power of Black Music: Interpreting Its History from Africa to the United States.* New York: Oxford University Press, 1995.

Fox, Ted. Press release. New York, 1988.

———. *In the Groove: The People Behind the Music.* New York: St. Martin's Press, 1986.

Fry, Macon, and Julie Posner. *Cajun Country Guide.* Gretna, LA: Pelican Publishing Co., 1992.

Gould, Philip. *Cajun Music and Zydeco.* Introduction by Barry Jean Ancelet. Baton Rouge: Louisiana State University Press, 1992.

Gregory, Hugh. *Soul Music A–Z.* New York: Da Capo Press, 1995.

Hall, Gwendolyn Midlo. *Africans in Colonial Louisiana: The Development of Afro-Creole Culture in the Eighteenth Century.* Baton Rouge: Louisiana State University Press, 1992.

Harris, Sheldon. *Blues Who's Who.* New York: Da Capo Press, 1989.

Hunt, Alfred N. *Haiti's Influence on Antebellum America: Slumbering Volcano in the Caribbean.* Baton Rouge: Louisiana State University Press, 1988.

Jackson, Bruce. *"Get Your Ass in the Water and Swim like Me": Narrative Poetry from Black Oral Tradition.* Cambridge, MA: Harvard University Press, 1974.

Lindahl, Carl, and Carolyn Ware. *Cajun Mardi Gras Masks.* Jackson: University Press of Mississippi, 1997.

Lomax, Alan. *The Land Where the Blues Began.* New York: Pantheon Books, 1993.

Nyhan, Pat, Brian Rollins, and David Babb. *Let the Good Times Roll! A Guide To Cajun & Zydeco Music.* Portland, ME: Upbeat Books, 1997.

Orlean, Susan. *Saturday Night.* New York: Alfred A. Knopf, 1990.

Rolling Stone, no. 27, February 15, 1969, page 8.

Savoy, Ann Allen. *Cajun Music: A Reflection of a People.* Vol. 1. Eunice, LA: The Bluebird Press, Inc., 1984.

Smith, Arthur L., ed. *Language, Communication and Rhetoric in Black America.* New York: Harper and Row, 1972.

Spitzer, Nicholas R., communication with author, 1998.

———. *Everything I'm Telling You Ain't No Lie: Down the Big Road with Boogie Bill Webb.* Chicago: Flying Fish Records/Baton Rouge: The Louisiana Folklife Recording Series (an extensive booklet that accompanies a long-play album). 1989.

———. "Zydeco and Mardi Gras: Creole Performance Genres and Identity in Rural French Louisiana." Ph.D. diss., University of Texas, 1986.

———. *Zodico: Louisiana Creole Music.* Somerville, MA: Rounder Records, 1979 (an extensive booklet that accompanies a long-play album).

———. *La La: Louisiana Black French Music.* Ville Platte, LA: Maison de Soul Records, 1977 (an extensive booklet that accompanies a long-play album).

Tisserand, Michael. *The Kingdom of Zydeco.* New York: Arcade Publishing, 1998.

Watrous, Peter. "A Raucous Brand of Zydeco Music." *New York Times,* May 23, 1990, section c, page 13.

Interviews

August, Lynn. Interview by author. Tape recording. Lafayette, LA, 1990.

Bonner, James "Sugarfoot." Telephone conversation with author. Tape recording. 1990.

Broussard, John. Interview by author. Tape recording. Lafayette, LA, 1989.

Ceasar, Warren. Interviews by author. Tape recording. Carencro, LA, 1987, 1988.

Chavis, Boozoo. Interview by author and Amanda LaFleur. Tape recording. Lake Charles, LA, 1987.

——. Interview by Haydée Lafaye Ellis. Tape recording. Lake Charles, LA, 1995. Excerpted from the series *The Creole Gumbo Radio Show,* © 1995 by the Abita Music Company. All rights reserved.

Chenier, C. J. Telephone conversation with author. Tape recording. 1995.

Chenier, Clifton. Interview by Barry Ancelet. Tape recording. University of Southwestern Louisiana, Center for Louisiana Studies, Lafayette, LA, circa 1986.

——. Interview by author. Tape recording. Lafayette, LA, 1983.

Crowell, Rodney. Telephone conversation with author, August 1998.

Delafose, Geno, and John Delafose. Telephone conversations with author. Tape recording. 1992.

Doucet, Michael. Telephone conversation with author, August 1998.

Dural, Stanley "Buckwheat." Interview by author. Tape recording. Metairie, LA, 1987.

Eaglin, Snooks. Interview by author. Tape recording. New Orleans, LA, 1989.

Fontenot, Canray. Interview by Jerry Embree. Tape recording. Welsh, LA, 1995. Excerpted from the series *The Creole Gumbo Radio Show,* © 1995 by the Abita Music Company. All rights reserved.

Guillory, Wilbert. Interview by author. Tape recording. Opelousas, LA, 1987.

Scott, Paul. Telephone conversation with author, 1998.

Simien, Rockin' Sidney. Telephone conversation with author. Tape recording. 1986.

Simien, Terrance. Interviews by author. Tape recordings. Mallet, LA, and Metairie, LA, 1987, 1990.

Soileau, Floyd. Interview by author. Tape recording. Ville Platte, LA, 1994.

Spitzer, Nick. Letter to author, 1998.

Williams, Nathan, and Sid Williams. Interviews by author. Tape recordings. Lafayette, LA, 1989.

Zydeco Information on the Internet

These principal sites provide links to many others

Gary Hayman's ZydE-Magic Cajun/Zydeco Web Page (http://www.nmaa.org/member/ghayman)

The Cajun & Creole Pages (http://http.tamu.edu:8000/~skb8721/

All Music Guide (http://allmusic.com)

Offbeat Magazine (http://www.offbeat.com)

Recommended Listening

Abshire, Nathan, *A Cajun Legend . . .* The Best of Nathan Abshire (Swallow SW 6061)

Adcock, C. C., *C. C. Adcock* (Island 314–518–840)

Angelle, Donna, *"Old Man's Sweetheart"* (Maison de Soul MdS-1067)

Arceneaux, Fernest, *Zydeco Blues Party* (Mardi Gras) MG 1019

Ardoin, Amédé, *The Roots of Zydeco* (Arhoolie/Folklyric CD 7007)

Ardoin, Alphonse "Bois Sec," with Canray Fontenot, *La Musique Creole* (Arhoolie CD 445)

Ardoin, Alphonse "Bois Sec," with Balfa Toujours, *Allons Danser* (Rounder CD 6081)

Ardoin, Chris, and Double Clutchin', *That's Da Lick!* (Maison de Soul MdS 1051)

———, *Lick It Up!* (Maison de Soul MdS 1058)

Arnold, Kokomo, *Casey Bill Weldon & Kokomo Arnold: Bottleneck Guitar Trendsetters of the 1930s* (Yazoo 1049)

August, Lynn, *Creole Cruiser* (Black Top BT-1074)

———, *Sauce Piquante* (Black Top BT-1092)

Balfa, Dewey, *The Balfa Brothers Play Traditional Cajun Music* (Swallow SW 6011)

Balfa, Dewey, and Friends, *Fait a la main* (Swallow SW 6063)

Ball, Marcia, *Hot Tamale Baby* (Rounder CD 3095)

BeauSoleil, *Parlez-nous a boire* (Arhoolie 322)

———, *L'amour ou la folie* (Rhino/Forward R2 72622)

Brooks, Lonnie, *Bayou Lightning* (Alligator ALCD 4714)

Brown, Clarence "Gatemouth," *The Original Peacock Recordings* (Rounder CD 2039)

Brown, James, *Star Time* (Polydor 849–108)

Buckwheat Zydeco, *Buckwheat's Zydeco Party* (Rounder CD 11528)

———, *Menagerie* (Mango 162–539–929)

———, *On a Night Like This* (Island 7567–90622)

———, *The Best of Louisiana Zydeco* (AVI CD 5011)

———, *Trouble* (Tomorrow Recording Company) (TMR 70001)

Carrier, Chubby, and the Bayou Swamp Band, *Who Stole the Hot Sauce?* (Blind Pig BPCD 5032)

Carrier, Roy, and the Night Rockers, *Twist & Shout* (Right on Rhythm ROR002)

Ceasar, Warren, and the Creole Zydeco Snap Band, *The Crowd Pleaser* (Sound of New Orleans SONO-1035)

Charles, Ray, *Genius & Soul* —The 50th . . . (WEA/Atlantic/Rhino 72859)

Chavis, Boozoo, *Boozoo Chavis* (Elektra/Nonesuch American Explorer Series 9–61146)

———, *Zydeco Homebrew* (Maison de Soul MdS 1028)

Chavis, Boozoo, and Nathan Williams, *Zydeco Live!* (Rounder CD 2069)

Chenier, C. J., and the Red Hot Louisiana Band, *My Baby Don't Wear No Shoes*
(Arhoolie CD 1098)

——, *Too Much Fun* (Alligator ALCD 4844)

Chenier, Clifton, *Louisiana Blues & Zydeco* (Arhoolie CD 329)

——, *The King of Zydeco Live at Montreux* (Arhoolie CD 355)

——, *Zydeco Dynamite: The Clifton Chenier Anthology* (Rhino R2 71194)

Chenier, Clifton, and the Red Hot Louisiana Band, *Bogalusa Boogie* (Arhoolie CD 347)

——, *I'm Here!* (Alligator ALCD 4729)

Chenier, Clifton, and Rod Bernard, *Boogie in Black and White* (JIN 9014, cassette
only)

Delafose, Geno, *French Rockin' Boogie* (Rounder 2131)

Delafose, Geno, and French Rockin' Boogie, *That's What I'm Talkin' About!* (Rounder
CD 2141)

Delafose, John, and the Eunice Playboys, *Heartaches and Hot Steps* (Maison de Soul
MdS 1035)

——, *Joe Pitre Got Two Women* (Arhoolie CD 335)

Delafose, John, and the Eunice Playboys/Willis Prudhomme and the Zydeco Express,
Zydeco Live! (Rounder CD 2070)

Delafose, John, featuring Geno Delafose, *Père et Garçon Zydeco* (Rounder CD 2116)

Domino, Fats, *They Call Me the Fat Man* (EMI CDP-7-96785)

Earth Wind & Fire, *Greatest Hits* (Sony 65779)

Fields, Thomas "Big Hat," and his Foot Stomping Zydeco Band, *Come to Louisiana*
(Lanor LN 1051)

Flatt, Lester, and Earl Scruggs, *At Carnegie Hall* (Koch KOC-CD-7929)

Fontenot, Canray, *Louisiana Hot Sauce* (Arhoolie CD 381)

Frank, Keith, *Only the Strong Survive* (Maison de Soul MdS 1062)

——, *What's His Name?* (Maison de Soul MdS 1053)

Fulson, Lowell, *The Complete Chess Masters* (Uni-Chess 9394)

Harpo, Slim, *The Best of Slim Harpo* (Rhino R2 71069)

Henry, Patrick, and the Liberation Band, *Come and Get It* (Lanor LN 1053)

Hopkins, Lightnin', *The Gold Star Sessions* (Arhoolie CD 330)

Jocque, Beau, and the Zydeco Hi-Rollers, *Beau Jocque Boogie* (Rounder CD 2120)

——, *Git It, Beau Jocque!* (Rounder CD 2134)

Jordan, Louis, *The Best of Louis Jordan* (UNI/MCA 4079)

King, B. B., *Live at the Regal* (UNI/MCA 11646)

Landreth, Sonny, *South of I-10* (Zoo Praxis 31070)

Ledet, Rosie, *Sweet Brown Sugar* (Maison de Soul, MdS 1052)

L'il Bob and the Lollipops, *Nobody But You* (La Louisianne LL-113, available on LP
only)

L'il Brian and the Zydeco Travelers, *Fresh* (Rounder CD 2136)

——, *Z-Funk* (Rounder CD 2146)

L'il Malcolm & the House Rockers, *L'il Malcolm & the House Rockers* (Maison de Soul MdS 1059)

Morton, Jelly Roll, *Kansas City Stomp* (Rounder CD 1091)

Mullican, Moon, *22 Greatest Hits* (Deluxe 7813)

Nathan and the Zydeco Cha-Chas, *Steady Rock* (Rounder CD 2092)

——, *I'm a Zydeco Hog* (Rounder CD 2143)

——, *Your Mama Don't Know* (Rounder CD 2107)

Nathan and the Zydeco Cha-Chas with Michael Doucet, *Creole Crossroads* (Rounder CD 2137)

Ohio Players, *Funk on Fire* (Polygram 528102)

Parliament/Funkadelic, *Uncut Funk—The Bomb: Parliament's Greatest Hits* (Casablanca/PolyGram 822 637)

Paul, J., Jr., and the Zydeco Newbreeds, *Taking Over* (Maison de Soul MdS 1066)

Richard, Belton, *The Essential Belton Richard* (Swallow SW 6117)

Richard, Zachary, *Zack's Bon Ton* (Rounder CD 6027)

Riley, Steve, and the Mamou Playboys, *La Toussaint* (Rounder CD 6068)

Rockin' Dopsie, *Crown Prince of Zydeco* (Maison de Soul MdS 1020, cassette only)

Rockin' Sidney, *My Toot Toot* (Maison de Soul MdS 1009)

Rodgers, Jimmie, *Train Whistle Blues* (Koch KOC-CD-7989)

Simon, Paul, *Graceland* (Warner Brothers 9362–46430)

Taylor, Jude, and His Burning Flames, *Best of Zydeco* (Mardi Gras 5011)

Toups, Wayne, *ZydeCajun* (PolyGram 846584)

Simien, Terrance, *There's Room for Us All* (Black Top BT 1096)

Snoop Dogg, *Da Game Is To Be Sold, Not To Be Told* (No Limit/Priority 50000)

Turner, Big Joe, *The Very Best of* (WEA/Atlantic/Rhino 72968)

Webster, Katie, *The Swamp Boogie Queen* (Alligator ALCD 4766)

Wheatstraw, Peetie, *The Devil's Son-in-Law, 1930-1941* (Story of Blues 3541)

Williams, Hank, *Low Down Blues* (Mercury 314-532-737)

Wills, Bob, and His Texas Playboys, *The Tiffany Transcriptions, Vol. 5* (Rhino R2 71473)

Zydeco Force, *The Zydeco Push* (Maison de Soul, MdS 1048)

Anthologies

Louisiana Cajun and Creole Music, 1934: The Lomax Recordings (Swallow SW LP-8003). Available on LP only, this two-album set presents a wealth of Creole and Cajun music, including such striking *juré* performances as "J'ai fait tout le tour du pays." This song is also available on CD, under the title "Zydeco sont pas salés" on *J'ai été au bal (I Went to the Dance)* (Arhoolie CD 332).

Louisiana Creole Music (Smithsonian Folkways, SFW 02622). Available by special order on recordable CD.

La-La, Louisiana Black French Music (Maison de Soul, MdS 1004). Available on LP only, this set of mid-1970s field recordings features Bébé and Eraste Carriere and Delton Broussard and the Lawtell Playboys.

La Musique de la Maison (Smithsonian Folkways, forthcoming SFW 40109)

Soca Music from Trinidad — "Heat In De Place" (Rounder CD 5041)

Zodico, Louisiana Creole Music (Rounder 6009). Available on LP only, this set of mid-1970s field recordings includes a capella chants and ballads as well rural zydeco.

Zouk Attack (Rounder CD 5037)

Zydeco: The Early Years (Arhoolie CD 307) includes Clarence Garlow's "Bon Ton Roula" and other seminal material.

Zydeco Shootout at El Sid O's (Rounder CD 2108) features live performances by Lynn August, Warren Ceasar, Zydeco Force, Jude Taylor, and others.

The R & B Box, 30 Years of Rhythm & Blues (Rhino R2 71806)

Swamp Gold, Volumes 1–5 (Jin 106, 107, 9041, 9042, 9053). A five-volume treasury of swamp pop.

The Chess Blues Box (MCA/Chess CHD4-9340). Features such influential Chicago artists as Muddy Waters, Howlin' Wolf, Little Walter, and Willie Dixon.

Films and Videos

Buckwheat Zydeco: Taking It Home (Island Records, 1990, directed by Bob Portway)

Cajun Visits/Les Blues de Balfa (Flower Films, 1983, directed by Yasha Aginsky). Includes footage of Canray Fontenot, Rockin' Dopsie, and Dewey Balfa.

Clifton Chenier: The King of Zydeco (Arhoolie Records, 1987, directed by Chris Strachwitz)

Dedans le Sud de la Louisiane (Cote blanche, 1983, directed by Jean-Pierre Bruneau). Includes footage of Bois-sec Ardoin, Canray and Bee Fontenot, and Clifton and Cleveland Chenier.

Dry Wood (Flower Films, 1979, directed by Les Blank). A documentary about Alphonse "Bois-sec" Ardoin.

Hot Pepper (Flower Films, 1973, directed by Les Blank). A documentary about Clifton Chenier.

J'ai été au bal (Flower Films, 1998, directed by Les Blank). Includes footage of Queen Ida, Rockin' Sidney, Boozoo Chavis, and Canray Fontenot.

The Kingdom of Zydeco (BMG Video, 1994, directed by Robert Mugge). Includes footage of Beau Jocque, Boozoo Chavis, Sid and Nathan Williams, and John Delafose.

Les créoles (National Film Board of Canada, 1983, in French, directed by Andre Gladu). Includes footage of Delton Broussard, Bébé Carrière, and ballad singer Inez Catalon.

Passion Fish (Miramax, 1992, directed by John Sayles), Includes great footage of John Delafose at Slim's Y-Ki-Ki.

Zarico (National Film Board of Canada, 1984, directed by André Gladu). Includes footage of Morris and Bois-sec Ardoin, Canray Fontenot, Ambrose Sam, Rockin' Dopsie, and Ann Goodly.

Zydeco (Flower Films, 1984, directed by Nick Spitzer and Steven Duplantier). Includes footage of Bébé Carrière, Bois-sec Ardoin, and *juré* singers.

Zydeco Gumbo (Rhapsody Films, 1990, directed by Dan Hildebrandt). Includes footage of Clifton Chenier and Beau Jocque.

Zydeco Nite 'n' Day (Island Films, 1991, directed by Robert Dowling, produced by Karen Andersen). Includes footage of Clifton Chenier, Rockin' Dopsie, Boozoo Chavis, and others.

Live Performances in Louisiana

The best-known and most atmospheric zydeco nightspots are centered around Lafayette, Louisiana. They include El Sid O's (318-237-1959) and Hamilton's (318-984-5583) in Lafayette, Slim's Y-Ki-Ki in Opelousas (318-942-9980), Richard's in Lawtell (318-543-6596), the Dauphine Club in Parks (318-394-9616), and the Offshore Lounge in Lawtell (318-543-9996, 543-7359). Schedules vary; performances are generally restricted to weekends. For information on the annual Southwest Louisiana Zydeco Festival, held on the Saturday of Labor Day weekend, call 318-942-2392.

Zydeco venues in New Orleans include the Maple Leaf (504-866-9359), Mid-City Bowling Lanes (504-482-3133), and House of Blues (504-529-2624.) The New Orleans Jazz & Heritage Festival, held annually from the last weekend in April through the first weekend in May, presents many zydeco artists; for information call 504-522-4786.

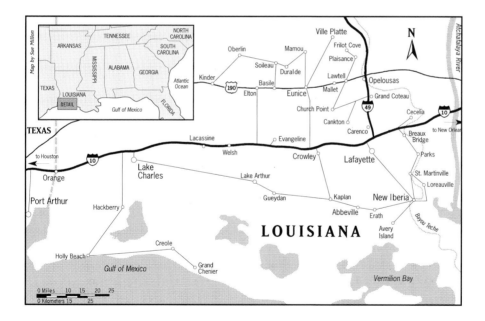

Song Credits

"Bad by Myself" (P. L. Grant II) Flat Town Music, BMI and Mike Lachney Music, BMI. Reprinted by permission.

"Bon Ton Rouleau" (Clarence Garlow, Eddie Shuler) Trio Music Company, Inc., BMI and Fort Knox Music, BMI. Used by permission.

Deacon John" (Wilson "Boozoo" Chavis) Flat Town Music, BMI. Reprinted by permission.

"Dog Hill" (Wilson "Boozoo" Chavis, Sidney Simien) Sid-Sim Music, BMI

"Dolomite" (anonymous) traditional

"I'm Here!" (Clifton Chenier) Stainless Music, BMI

"La valse de Holly Beach" (Nathan Abshire) Flat Town Music, BMI. Reprinted by permission.

"Let's Do the Zydeco" (Clifton Chenier) Stainless Music, BMI

"Night Train" (Jimmy Forrest, Oscar Washington) Embassy Music, BMI. Reprinted by permission.

"Old Man's Sweetheart" (Donna Angelle, Michelle Citizen, Mike Lachney) Flat Town Music, BMI and Mike Lachney Music, BMI. Reprinted by permission.

"Uncle Bud" (Wilson "Boozoo" Chavis) Flat Town Music, BMI

"What My Mama Told Me" (Amos Blakemore [Junior Wells]) Bluesharp Music, BMI

"Zydeco Hee Haw" (Wilson "Boozoo" Chavis) Flat Town Music, BMI. Reprinted by permission.

"Zydeco sont pas salés" (Clifton Chenier) Tradition Music, BMI, administered by Bug Music Company. Reprinted by permission.

The fieldwork recordings from Rodrigue were made by Jean-Pierre LaSelve, and were transcribed and translated by Barry Ancelet. The tapes are in the archives of the University of Southwest Louisiana Center for Acadian and Creole Folklore, in Lafayette, Louisiana.

Acknowledgments

A hearty *merci beaucoup* to all the zydeco musicians and their families and friends and to the club owners and their associates, without whom this work would not have been possible. To welcome an outsider (especially one with a camera) with a spirit of warmth and generosity is the mark of a truly outstanding group of people. I will always be grateful and indebted to all who took time out to show me the beauty of their life, land, and music.

Rick Olivier

Thanks for the encouragement, help, suggestions, and information to the following people: Caroline Ancelet, Miriam Altshuler, Christine Baer, Cary Baker, Marcia Ball, Shane Bernard, Warren Ceasar, Rodney Crowell, Quint Davis, Michael and Sharon Doucet, Louis Edwards, Steve and Haydée Ellis, Jerry Embree, Greg Eveline Juwanda Ford, John Fox, Ted Fox, Herman Fuselier, Mindy Giles, Pete Gregory, Wilbert Guillory, Jeff Hannusch, Tamarin Hennebury, Mary Howell, Tad Jones, Ann Kennedy, Malise Kerrigan, Sandy LaBry, Mike Lachney, Karen Leipziger, Daniel Levine, Susan Levitas, Alice Lieberman, Melanie McKay, Elemore Morgan, Jr., Echo Olander, the late Robert Palmer, Tom Piazza, Jerry Rappaport, Francis and Cathi Pavy, Clare Beth Pierson, Ellen Pryor, Chris Rose, Mark Satlof, Marc and Ann Savoy, Paul Scott, Liz Schoenberg, Lisa Shively, Floyd Soileau, Chris Strachwitz, Liz Thiels, the Williams family—Sid and Suzanne, Nathan and Nancy, and Dennis—and Tracy Wright.

Special thanks to Philip Gould for many nights on the zydeco trail; Peter Guralnick for years of good advice; Don McLeese for sage counsel to a rookie writer; Amanda LaFleur for providing translations and charming Mr. Chavis; Susan Millon for creating the map; Joe Regal at Russell & Volkening for taking this to Mississippi and to JoAnne Prichard, editor, for bringing it into focus; Nick Spitzer for expert scrutiny of several sections and many miscellaneous answers; Michael Tisserand for "zyde-codependecy"; Lucian K. Truscott IV for the introduction to Russell & Volkening.

Special thanks also to Bruce Iglauer for the Clifton Chenier liner-notes assignment; Scott Billington and David Bither for the zydeco liner-notes assignments that followed; and the magazine editors who published my zydeco articles, including Connie Atkinson at *Wavelength*, Pat Clinton at *The Reader*, Bruce Eggler at the New Orleans *Times-Picayune*, Howard Mandel at *Down Beat*, Nancy Marshall at *Louisiana Life*, Laurie Macintosh at *Pulse!*, Mark Rowland at *Musician*, and William Whitworth at *The Atlantic Monthly*.

Eternal gratitude to Karen Celestan, Judith Levine, Sydney Lewis, and Nancy Sternberg for eagle-eyeing the manuscript and to Barry Ancelet for reading it all, making crucial comments, and patiently fielding questions.

Ben Sandmel

Index

Rick Olivier is an award-winning New Orleans photographer whose work has been internationally exhibited and is part of the permanent collections of both the New Orleans Museum of Art and the Historic New Orleans Collection. **Ben Sandmel** is a folklorist and the zydeco programming consultant for the New Orleans Jazz & Heritage Festival. He is also the producer and drummer for the Grammy-nominated Cajun band, the Hackberry Ramblers. Olivier and Sandmel's work has appeared in such publications as *Rolling Stone, Esquire, The Atlantic Monthly,* and *The New York Times Magazine,* and they have provided the photography and liner notes for numerous zydeco albums.

Rick Olivier (left) and Ben Sandmel
Photo by Aimeé Toledano